Cambridge Elements ≡

Elements in Public and Nonprofit Administration
edited by
Andrew Whitford
University of Georgia
Robert Christensen
Brigham Young University

COURT-ORDERED COMMUNITY SERVICE

The Experiences of Community Organizations and Community Service Workers

Rebecca Nesbit
University of Georgia

Su Young Choi
University of Georgia

Jody Clay-Warner
University of Georgia

Shaftesbury Road, Cambridge CB2 8EA, United Kingdom

One Liberty Plaza, 20th Floor, New York, NY 10006, USA

477 Williamstown Road, Port Melbourne, VIC 3207, Australia

314–321, 3rd Floor, Plot 3, Splendor Forum, Jasola District Centre, New Delhi – 110025, India

103 Penang Road, #05–06/07, Visioncrest Commercial, Singapore 238467

Cambridge University Press is part of Cambridge University Press & Assessment, a department of the University of Cambridge.

We share the University's mission to contribute to society through the pursuit of education, learning and research at the highest international levels of excellence.

www.cambridge.org
Information on this title: www.cambridge.org/9781009631730

DOI: 10.1017/9781009631778

First published 2024

A catalogue record for this publication is available from the British Library

ISBN 978-1-009-63173-0 Hardback
ISBN 978-1-009-63172-3 Paperback
ISSN 2515-4303 (online)
ISSN 2515-429X (print)

Cambridge University Press & Assessment has no responsibility for the persistence or accuracy of URLs for external or third-party internet websites referred to in this publication and does not guarantee that any content on such websites is, or will remain, accurate or appropriate.

Court-Ordered Community Service

The Experiences of Community Organizations and Community Service Workers

Elements in Public and Nonprofit Administration

DOI: 10.1017/9781009631778
First published online: December 2024

Rebecca Nesbit
University of Georgia

Su Young Choi
University of Georgia

Jody Clay-Warner
University of Georgia

Author for correspondence: Rebecca Nesbit, nesbit7@uga.edu

Abstract: Community service is a common court-ordered sanction in many countries. Individuals sentenced to community service must work a specified number of uncompensated hours at an approved community agency, typically as a condition of probation. A core expectation of court-ordered community service is that the community agencies benefit from this labor. However, very little research examines the organizational and interpersonal dynamics involved when community organizations work with court-ordered community service workers. What are local public and nonprofit organizations' experiences with court-ordered community service workers? How do the workers, themselves, experience court-ordered community service within community agencies? This Element addresses these questions through interviews with thirty-one volunteer managers and thirty-four court-ordered community service workers in two court jurisdictions in northeast Georgia. The Element frames its findings within the volunteer management literature and suggests practices that could improve experiences for both the court-ordered community service worker and the community organization.

Keywords: probation, community service work, volunteer management, court-ordered volunteers, court-mandated community service

ISBNs: 9781009631730 (HB), 9781009631723 (PB), 9781009631778 (OC)
ISSNs: 2515-4303 (online), 2515-429X (print)

Contents

1 Background and Theoretical Foundations

Court-ordered community service is a common condition of probation in many Western countries. Those sentenced to court-ordered community service are required to work for a specified number of hours without pay for approved nonprofit or governmental organizations (Carter et al., 1987; Harland, 1980; Pease, 1985). Community service work may be implemented either as a stand-alone punishment or alongside other so-called alternative sanctions, such as restitution, intensive monitoring, and fines (Carter et al., 1987). There is considerable variability in the type of labor that court-ordered community service workers (CSWs) perform and in the number of hours required to complete their sentences. Uniformly, though, these workers perform conscripted labor for organizations with a public-serving mission and whose structure is built to accommodate a voluntary workforce. The incorporation of court-mandated CSWs into this structure may prove challenging for both the organization and the CSWs themselves.

While court-ordered community service programs have a number of different goals, a consistent product of these programs has been the provision of labor to community organizations (Tonry, 1999). The "free labor" that CSWs provide, though, may come at a cost. Additional time is needed to supervise such workers, which can drain already-limited organizational resources. There are also additional paperwork demands and the need for ongoing communication with the probation office. Some CSWs might resent their sentence and be more challenging to motivate and supervise as a result. Staff and other volunteers might be resistant to working with CSWs. Some court jurisdictions also place restrictions on CSWs that are both stigmatizing to the workers and make it challenging for nonprofits to integrate CSWs into their organizations.

Given these issues, accepting CSWs presents several unique management challenges for community organizations. These challenges have not been adequately investigated. A few older empirical studies show that the agencies are generally appreciative of CSW's work and that CSWs are satisfied with the community service work program (Allen & Treger, 1990; McIvor, 1993a, 1993b). However, these studies provide very little insight into the dynamics of the relationship between community organizations and CSWs. These studies are also dated, and only one was conducted in the US (Allen & Treger, 1990), where we focus our attention.

Even less research has considered court-ordered community service from the perspective of the CSW. While a few studies have examined the validity of community service as an alternative to incarceration (Bouffard & Muftic, 2006; Feeley et al., 1992; Harland, 1980), there is limited literature examining how CSWs, themselves, feel about the sanction and the organizations for whom they work. We also have little information about the ways in which these workers interact with the staff, other volunteers, and clients of the community agencies. This is a notable gap, as one ostensible goal of requiring community service work is to help the worker reintegrate into the community (Bazemore, 1991; Brown, 1977; Klein, 1982). We cannot know if this is even a reasonable goal without talking to the CSWs about their experiences.

To investigate these issues, we interviewed thirty-one managers at thirty nonprofit and public agencies working with CSWs. We also interviewed thirty-four CSWs about their attitudes toward community service and their experiences doing their community service work. Our study sites are two court jurisdictions in northeast Georgia.

In order to understand our findings, however, it is necessary to understand the role of court-ordered community service in the US criminal legal system. We begin by providing an overview of the larger probation system in which court-ordered community service operates and then discuss the role of court-ordered community service in the US as a common condition of probation. We then describe the history and goals of court-ordered community service and prior empirical research on the topic.

1.1 Probation in the US Criminal Legal System

The US criminal legal system is composed of overlapping local, state, and federal jurisdictions (for an overview, see Hart, 1954). Each state system operates independently from all other state systems, as well as from the federal system, which results in variability in courts' policies governing sentencing. At the same time, federal civil rights law ultimately dictates the conditions of punishment that states can exert on inmates (The Civil Rights of Institutionalized Persons Act (CRIPA), 42 U.S.C. § 1997a). States also frequently look to other states when making decisions about their own legal systems, a process known as isomorphism (DiMaggio & Powell, 2010; Rubin, 2015). As a result, there are many common threads running through the overlapping court systems that enact criminal punishment in the US.

In the US criminal legal system, regardless of jurisdiction, judges make sentencing decisions following either a guilty plea or a conviction. For more severe offenses, the range of sentences available to a judge is often determined by state or federal law (U.S. Sentencing Commission, 2023). For example, many states have codified mandatory minimums for serious violent crimes, such as robbery, rape, and homicide. Likewise, persons convicted of certain federal drug offenses are also subject to a mandatory period of incarceration (U.S. Sentencing Commission, 2023).

Judges typically have a great deal of discretion, however, in determining punishments for less serious crimes. For minor offenses, such as public order offenses and low-level property crimes, judges may choose to sentence offenders to probation either in lieu of jail or following a period of incarceration. During the period of probation, the offender remains under the supervision of the criminal legal system and is required to satisfy a set of predetermined conditions. The probation conditions vary by the nature of the crime committed and the circumstances of the offender, but these conditions may include reporting monthly to a probation officer, paying a fine or restitution, getting treatment for a drug or alcohol problem, maintaining a curfew, or going to counseling. Probation is administered by a probation office – either a government agency or a private contractor. Probation officers are assigned to meet with each offender consistently and to ensure that the conditions of probation are being met. Violation of the conditions of probation can result in the offender receiving additional sanctions, being put in jail, and/or returning to court.

Though probation is often seen as a lower-cost punishment that is also advantageous to offenders, a growing literature challenges these assumptions (Phelps, 2020). Probation conditions are intrusive and time-consuming (Doherty, 2016), and even minor technical violations – such as missing an appointment with the probation officer or inability to pay probation fees – can lead to a longer sentence, a return to court, and/or jail time (Klingele, 2013). Probation also extends the period of criminal justice supervision, a period in which probation officers have a great deal of power over offenders' lives. In addition, when probation is a stand-alone punishment, it often results in net-widening, which is the process of extending criminal justice sanctions that are intended to serve as an alternative to incarceration to those who would not have been subject to incarceration, thus widening the net of criminal justice control. Probation is often cited as an example of net-widening, as many who are given a probation sentence are convicted of offenses for which jail time is unlikely (Phelps, 2013). Due to net-widening, it is unclear how much cost savings are associated with the widespread use of probation. Despite these contradictions, probation continues to be a common sanction for low-level offending, with court-ordered community service a common condition of probation.

1.2 History of Court-Ordered Community Service in Europe

The roots of court-ordered community service are generally traced to the Wootten Report on alternatives to incarceration (Home Office, 1970), which was commissioned by the UK government (Pease, 1985). The report advocated for court-ordered community service as an alternative to incarceration and provided recommendations for its use. These recommendations were modified and ultimately codified into the Criminal Justice Act of 1972 (Pease, 1985). The Act stipulated that the courts could only order community service for crimes that were punishable by incarceration, as community service was intended as a true alterative to imprisonment. The Act also specified that only those at least sixteen years of age could be sentenced to community service and that they must be sentenced for between 40 and 240 hours, all of which must be completed within one year. Unlike the systems of court-ordered community service that emerged in the US, community service was not part of a probation sentence in the UK but was, instead, a stand-alone punishment.

Following its adoption in the UK, Western European countries also began to use court-ordered community service. The Netherlands adopted it first in 1981 as an alternative to incarceration and used community service in a very similar way as it is used in the US. In the Netherlands, court-ordered community service is technically reserved only for those who would otherwise be sentenced to prison for up to six months (Spaans, 1998). Evidence suggests, though, that the actual implementation of community service in the Netherlands has produced a net-widening effect, as it has been used as a replacement for less serious non-imprisonment sentences, including suspended sentences (Spaans, 1998). In 1982, Denmark became the first Scandinavian country to begin using community service, with the other Scandinavian countries not joining until the 1990s (Dünkel & Lappi-Seppälä, 2014). Finland started to use it on an experimental basis in 1991, making it a permanent part of the legal code in 1997 (Muiluvuori, 2001), while penal reforms in the 2000s further increased its use in Sweden (Dünkel & Lappi-Seppälä, 2014). Court-ordered community service is now used on a widespread basis across Western Europe.

1.3 History of Court-Ordered Community Service in the United States

In the 1970s, judges and court systems in the United States began implementing community service as a condition of probation, partly due to its popularity in the United Kingdom (Harland, 1980; McIvor, 2016; Pease, 1985). A working draft of the Federal Criminal Code Revision Act of 1979 formally recognized community service as an acceptable condition of probation, and since then, interest in – and use of – community service has burgeoned (Harland, 1980). Throughout the late 1970s and 1980s, many states adopted statutes and policies permitting the use of community service as a condition of probation. Federal law 18 U.S.C. § 3563(b)(12) provides the courts with the authority to require a defendant to "work in community service as directed by the court."

The earliest documented use of court-ordered community service in the US was in Alameda County, California, in the late 1960s. This was a very limited program, though, that offered community service to female traffic violators who were unable to pay their fines so that they could avoid jail time for nonpayment (Wood, 2012). Following the initiation of community service in the UK in the early 1970s, community service became increasingly popular across the US (Tonry & Lynch, 1996). Unlike in the UK, however, in the US, community service has been largely seen as an intermediate sanction – a punishment somewhere between simple probation and incarceration – instead of as a true alternative to incarceration (Harland, 1980). Indeed, research suggests that community service in the US has led to greater net-widening despite evidence that it can be an effective diversionary tool (McDonald, 1986, 1988; Tonry, 1999).

Though court-ordered community service is common, it is difficult to obtain data on the extent of its use across the US because the US criminal legal system is composed of multiple jurisdictions, as previously described. Thus, up-to-date, comprehensive data are not available. One of the few comprehensive reports produced by the Bureau of Justice Statistics provides data on the use of community service in 1995. At that time, approximately 25 percent of the 1.5 million felons and one million misdemeanants under supervision in the United States had some kind of community service as part of their sentence (Bonczar, 1997).

Recent state-level reports on the use of community service indicate that large numbers of people participate in court-ordered community service programs. During the 2017–2018 fiscal year, for example, probationers in Florida completed 1.1 million hours of community service, which was equivalent to $11 million dollars of labor based on the state's minimum wage (Florida Department of Corrections 2017–18 Annual Report, 2018). In New York in 2015, 12,818 probationers were assigned community service (Executive Law Article 13-A Classification/Alternatives to Incarceration Program 2015 Annual Report, 2016). A study in Illinois reported that 32 percent of the approximately 1,100 sampled probationers were required to complete community service (Illinois Criminal Justice Information Authority, 2011). Although these few reports do not give a thorough accounting of the extent of court-ordered community service in the United States, they do give a sense of its scope while also indicating how little we actually know about community service as a criminal justice sanction.

1.4 Empirical Research on Court-Ordered Community Service

The limited empirical literature on court-ordered community service focuses primarily on outcomes related to the criminal justice system rather than on its impact on the organizations who work with CSWs. Such research has examined whether court-ordered community service saves money (e.g., Killias et al., 2000; Killias, Gilliéron, Kissling, et al., 2010; Killias, Gilliéron, Villard, et al., 2010; Knapp et al., 1992; McIvor et al., 2010; Schiff, 2003; Wermink et al., 2010), affects recidivism (e.g., Killias et al., 2000; Killias, Gilliéron, Kissling, et al., 2010; Killias, Gilliéron, Villard, et al., 2010; Schiff, 2003; Wermink et al., 2010), and has the potential to help CSWs reintegrate into the community (Gelsthorpe & Rex, 2004; Killias et al., 2000; McIvor, 1992; Rex & Gelsthorpe, 2002). These studies provide a mixed portrait of the effectiveness of community service, and taken together, this work reveals that we know little about the nature and outcomes of court-ordered community service, especially in the United States. The broader literature also finds critics on both sides of the aisle – liberals who see community service as net-widening and conservatives who see it as soft on crime (e.g., Cohen, 2008; Shichor, 2000).

Conversations about court-ordered community service, though, rarely consider how court-ordered community service affects the recipient community organizations or the CSWs themselves. This said, two studies conducted in Scotland in the early 1990s provide some insights. First, a survey of elderly and infirm individuals for whom court-ordered CSWs in Scotland performed household tasks revealed high levels of satisfaction with CSWs (McIvor, 1993a). Second, McIvor (1993a) surveyed 172 local organizations using CSWs in Scotland about their attitudes and experiences. The agencies reported generally high levels of satisfaction with the CSWs, although half the agencies reported problems with their workers, such as lack of motivation or effort, poor attendance, and lack of punctuality. These studies give us an idea of some of the issues that organizations may face in working with CSWs.

1.5 A Framework for Managing Court-Ordered Community Service Workers

We use the volunteer management literature to develop a conceptual framework to understand how community organizations manage CSWs. Community organizations typically delegate responsibility for supervising all nonpaid employees, including both volunteers and CSWs, to one individual – the volunteer manager. While there are different approaches to volunteer management (Brudney & Meijs, 2014), the most commonly discussed model in both the academic and practitioner literature is the human resources model. In this model, volunteer management mirrors the organization's human resource function and comprises such tasks as: planning, work design, recruitment, screening, onboarding, supervision, recognition, evaluation, and recordkeeping (Brudney,

2010; Connors, 2011; Gazley & Brudney, 2005; Hager & Brudney, 2004; Jackson et al., 2019; Machin & Paine, 2008; UPS Foundation, 2002).

Our conceptual framework is informed by the research literature on volunteer management and court-ordered community service. The framework consists of three phases of working with CSWs: (1) preparing for CSWs, (2) onboarding CSWs, and (3) creating a supportive environment. We briefly discuss the volunteer management practices within each phase and how they might be applied to working with CSWs.

1.5.1 Preparing for Community Service Workers

The first part of preparing for CSWs is that the organization needs to know why it is bringing in CSWs. Effective volunteer programs start with a rationale for volunteer involvement that describes why the organization uses volunteers and how they contribute to mission fulfillment (Connors, 2011; Jackson et al., 2019). The rationale serves as a framework for setting goals for the volunteer program, getting staff buy-in, and developing a strong volunteer management infrastructure (Nesbit, 2024). Volunteers who understand their roles within the organization and know how they contribute to the organization's goals are more satisfied and more likely to continue their volunteering (Hidalgo & Moreno, 2009), so it stands to reason that CSWs who know their roles will be more satisfied as well. But the important precursor is that organizations must be clear about what they hope to accomplish with CSWs.

Because organizations "recruit" CSWs from probation offices, a second part of preparing for CSWs is building a relationship with a probation office. Court-ordered community service must meet the needs and interests of the criminal legal system in addition to those of the community organization, so this relationship brings with it a new set of rules and procedures the organization must follow. At the very least, community organizations will need to keep accurate records so that they can report how many community service hours a CSW has completed. They will also need to maintain an ongoing relationship with the probation office in order to be informed of changes in rules, procedures, and policies and to receive help and support throughout the process. Prior research has shown that community agencies appreciate support and advice from the bureaucrats managing court-ordered community service (McIvor, 1993a). One survey of community agencies using CSWs found that they desired improved communication from the probation office and easier reporting procedures (Allen & Treger, 1990). The relationship between the community organization and the probation office could have significant consequences for the success of court-ordered community service – it could either place additional strain on community agencies or relieve some of their burdens.

Next, organizations must design the jobs and tasks that CSWs will perform. A well-designed volunteer job description helps an organization plan how to train and support a volunteer in a specific position, and it communicates clear expectations to volunteers (Brudney, 2016; Jackson et al., 2019). Volunteers want to do work that they find meaningful, meaning work that contributes to the good of the organization's beneficiaries or the organization itself (Dwyer et al., 2013; Grube & Piliavin, 2000). Volunteers who feel their work is meaningful are more satisfied and continue longer in their positions (Hobson, 2007; Kulik, 2006), whereas volunteers who do general labor have higher turnover than those doing more skills-based work (Eisner et al., 2009). Community service workers are not helping the organization voluntarily, so their primary motivation is to complete their community service hours. However, despite this motivation, it is likely that CSWs who have meaningful work will be more satisfied and might feel better about doing community service than those who do unpleasant manual labor.

The final part of preparing for CSWs is that organizations need to develop policies to provide guidance for onboarding and managing CSWs. Good volunteer programs have policies that guide volunteer behavior and staff behavior relative to volunteers (Jackson et al., 2019; Nesbit, 2024). Policies protect the organization and its stakeholders from unnecessary risk (Graff, 2012; Herman, 2021). Aside from basic criminal liability, this literature warns about potential harm to the organization's clients and other stakeholders, property or assets, or reputation (Graff, 2012). Prior research has shown that many community organizations refuse to accept CSWs convicted of certain crimes, such as violent crimes, sexual offenses, and crimes against children, due to the potential risk posed to clients and staff (McIvor, 1993a). Liability is among the top concerns for community organizations receiving CSWs (Allen & Treger, 1990). In response to these concerns, community organizations may adopt additional rules to mitigate risk, such as requiring open identification of CSWs while they are working onsite or limiting which offenses the organization accepts, what type of work CSWs perform, and CSWs' interactions with clients.

1.5.2 Onboarding Community Service Workers

Onboarding new volunteers begins with screening potential volunteers and matching them to specific positions in the organization. Organizations use screening procedures to optimize the match between the volunteer, the organization, and the work the volunteer will do (Meijs & Brudney, 2007). Screening helps organizations avoid common problems, such as unreliability or lacking the skills necessary for a particular job (Frenzel, 2021; Graff, 2012; Kyrwood &

Meneghetti, 2010). Typical screening procedures include an application, interview, and background or reference checks. In one survey of community organizations using CSWs, over half of the agencies reported some type of problem with their CSWs, such as poor attendance and lack of punctuality, which can increase the amount of staff time needed to manage them (McIvor, 1993a). Screening gives organizations an opportunity to screen out CSWs who might be difficult or unreliable workers.

The last part of onboarding is providing orientation and training. An orientation overviews the organization's mission, programs, and policies while training teaches volunteers the knowledge and skills they need for their particular role (Frenzel, 2021; Jackson et al., 2019; Kyrwood & Meneghetti, 2010). Familiarity with the organization shows the volunteers how what they do contributes to the organization's mission. Orientations are perhaps even more crucial for CSWs who might not have any prior familiarity with the organization and its mission and might not know how the organization contributes to the community. Community service workers will also need training so they know what to do and how to complete their tasks properly.

1.5.3 Creating a Supportive Environment

CSWs – just like volunteers – need supervision, communication, and support from a manager in order to be successful. Managers need to be available to answer volunteers' questions and provide them with feedback on their work. Volunteers want to know that they will be supported by their organization and that their time will be used effectively (Boezeman & Ellemers, 2008; Hasselmann, 2013; Kolnick & Mulder, 2007). Effective communication leads to positive volunteer outcomes, such as reduced turnover (Alfes et al., 2016; Farmer & Fedor, 2001; Hidalgo & Moreno, 2009; Hobson et al., 1997). Indeed, ineffective management is one of the reasons that volunteers quit their volunteering (Brodie et al., 2011). It is also important that CSWs receive appropriate supervision and communication so that their time is used well, and they make valuable contributions to the organization.

Relationships between staff and CSWs heavily determine whether CSWs are working in a supportive environment. The volunteer management literature highlights the importance of good relationships between volunteers and staff for a successful volunteer program (Jackson et al., 2019; MacDuff, 2012). Staff members' negative experiences with volunteers lead to stress, decreased job satisfaction, and increased turnover intentions (Bittschi et al., 2019; Rogelberg et al., 2010). Negative interpersonal relationships also increase volunteer turnover (Galindo-Kuhn & Guzley, 2001; Kulik, 2006). Sources of tension between staff and volunteers can include different expectations, communication challenges, interpersonal issues, and job vulnerability (Rimes et al., 2017). Given that strained relationships between organization staff and volunteers are not uncommon (Rimes et al., 2017; Rogelberg et al., 2010), it is reasonable to expect some staff resistance to working with CSWs and that cultural stigma associated with offender status would amplify this resistance (Hirschfield & Piquero, 2010; Uggen et al., 2014). Potential employers cited concerns about how staff and clients would respond to hiring and interacting with a formerly incarcerated individual and whether that individual had sufficient people skills to interact effectively with others (Giguere & Dundes, 2002). It is likely that staff will project similar stigma and concerns onto CSWs. In essence, due to CSWs' past crimes and due to the additional supervision burden already discussed, staff might be reluctant to work with CSWs, leading to strained relationships.

Finally, creating a supportive environment for CSWs means recognizing and thanking them for their contributions. The practitioner literature on volunteer management is replete with admonishments about the importance of volunteer recognition and methods for showing gratitude and appreciation to volunteers (Fallon & Rice, 2015; Graff, 2005). Volunteers who receive some type of recognition are more satisfied with their volunteer work and more likely to continue their volunteering (Kulik, 2006; Wisner et al., 2005). While CSWs do not complete community service voluntarily, even a simple thank you or other types of recognition can make CSWs feel more comfortable in the organization and can make them feel valued. Recognition can help CSWs to feel that they are doing work that benefits their community rather than just being punished.

We use this conceptual framework of the three phrases of involving CSWs – preparing, onboarding, and creating a supportive environment – to understand how volunteer management best practices can be used with CSWs. We seek to understand community organizations' experiences with CSWs, particularly through the lens of the volunteer manager – the individual responsible for onboarding and overseeing unpaid workers. We also want to understand how CSWs experience the community organizations and their community service work. We thus build on prior research to examine the management choices and dynamics within community organizations that accept CSWs while also exploring how CSWs feel about their interactions with these organizations. The primary research questions for this study are: What are local public and nonprofit organizations' experiences with CSWs? How do the CSWs themselves experience court-ordered community service within community organizations? We conclude by suggesting ways that organizations can improve their operations to make the organization/CSW relationship more mutually beneficial.

2 The Study

This exploratory study was conducted in two jurisdictions in the state of Georgia in the United States in Fall 2017 through Summer 2018. The study was approved by the University of Georgia's Institutional Review Board.

The 2017 annual report of the Georgia Department of Community Supervision (DCS) indicates that there were 253,843 offenders under DCS supervision, with an average load of 139 cases per probation officer (Georgia Department of Community Supervision, 2017). Across the United States, the number of adults in the United States on probation was 3,673,100 – or 1 in 68 adults – at the end of 2016 (Kaeble, 2018). Georgia is known for having a particularly large number of probationers – reported at 471,067 in 2014, partly due to the extensive use of private probation (Teegardin, 2015).

2.1 Partner Probation Offices

The research team partnered with two probation offices for this study. Both offices are located in the same judicial district in Georgia. We will call the first probation office, the Dogwood Office. This office serves one urban county. We will call the second office, the Azalea Office. This office serves three more rural counties. Both offices are responsible for supervising probationers within their jurisdiction, although the form and methods of supervising probationers vary across jurisdictions.

The Georgia DCS provides policy guidance for its offices overseeing probation (Georgia Department of Community Supervision, 2017). The officers select public and nonprofit agencies for the CSWs, who sign an agreement to abide by the community service program's policies. The probation office either selects a community service site for the probationer or allows them to select from a list of available organizations. According to DCS policy, felony offenders have three years to complete their community service hours, and misdemeanor offenders have twelve months. Probationers should complete a minimum average of sixteen hours per month, which averages to about four hours per week. The probation office can assign additional community service hours for a non-revocable offense or in lieu of a fine. Although the number of service hours required will vary by probationer and offense, there is some degree of commonality across judges for the same offense. For example, it is common for judges in this judicial district to assign 40 hours for the first DUI (driving under the influence) and 240 for the second DUI.

The Azalea Office faces a distinct set of challenges. The Azalea Office grapples with finding suitable agencies for community service across the three counties it serves, partly due to community demographics and the area's geographic size and rurality. Transportation issues, travel time, and probationers' work hours make it difficult for them to serve at the available locations. At the time of the study, the Azalea Office had eight community service locations – two government agencies and six nonprofits. Additionally, they would permit probationers to perform community service hours at the probation office. Indeed, sometimes they would require probationers to start their community service at their office when they felt that the probationers needed extra encouragement or supervision. At the time of the study, the Azalea Office had about 100 probationers with community service requirements.

The Dogwood Office is an independent probation office, created in 2008. In 2009, the Dogwood Office encountered problems with how community service was being administered in their area. Specifically, some county employees had been selling community service hours to probationers and reporting fraudulent time sheets. After that, the Dogwood Office created a stricter set of policies for its partner agencies and developed a training module that the person managing CSWs at each agency was required to attend. The Dogwood Office partners with twenty-two nonprofits on a regular basis and an additional five nonprofits that request CSWs for special events once or twice a year. The Office also partners with ten public agencies. At the time of the study, the Dogwood Office had approximately 1,500 active probationers.

2.2 Data Collection: Volunteer Managers

The first data collection involved semi-structured interviews with the employees managing the court-ordered CSWs at each agency. For most organizations, this person was also responsible for managing all the volunteers at that organization. The Azalea and Dogwood Offices provided the research team with the list of public and nonprofit organizations hosting CSWs, and a member of the research team reached out to each organization with an invitation to participate in the study. The research team hoped to interview the volunteer manager from all organizations on the list, but not all the organizations responded despite several requests for an interview. The final study included thirty-one interviews representing thirty organizations – twenty-five organizations partnering with the Dogwood Office (all located in one urban county) and six with the Azalea Office (spread across three more rural counties). Twenty-five interviewees represented nonprofits, and the other six were from public agencies. The research team conducted two interviews at one organization (a nonprofit) because the volunteer manager position had recently changed, so both the current and prior volunteer managers were interviewed. Organization names are withheld to honor our confidentiality agreement with the interviewees, and we use pseudonyms for the volunteer managers.

Most of the interviews with these managers were conducted between September and November 2017, but one additional interview was conducted in June 2018 when the research team followed up with each nonresponding organization. Interviews were conducted either on the phone or in-person, depending upon the preference of the interviewee. The interview questions addressed the background of the person managing the volunteers (e.g., length of time at the organization, experience managing volunteers), the organization's use of CSWs (e.g., the rationale for working with CSWs, what offenses they accept, their rules and policies around CSWs), questions about the CSWs themselves (e.g., their reliability and motivation, challenges in managing them, positive and negative experiences), and questions about the larger public purposes of community service (e.g., whether the service helps the probationers and whether it helps rehabilitate offenders). All interviews were recorded and transcribed.

2.3 Data Collection: Probationers

We also conducted semi-structured interviews with individuals on probation who had community service requirements, or CSWs. The inclusion criteria were that the individual had community service as part of their sentence and had completed at least ten hours of service. The probation offices were given the IRB-approved recruitment script. Probation officers at each location were asked to use the script to invite individuals to participate in the study when they had their regular probation meetings. The officers would then refer interested individuals to the research team. Interviewees were given a $15 Walmart gift card for participating in the interview. The final study data included interviews with thirty-four CSWs, eighteen supervised by the Dogwood Office and fourteen supervised by the Azalea Office. The CSWs are identified by pseudonyms.

The interviews were conducted in February and March 2018. Most of the interviews were conducted in person in a private room at the probation office, but thirteen were conducted on the phone. The questions for the semi-structured interviews included questions about where the community service was being done and the CSW's experience with the work (i.e., which organization, tasks completed, positive and negative experiences), the CSW's attitudes toward community service (i.e., motivation to complete hours, fairness, attitudes about community services as a policy tool), barriers to completing service hours, and volunteering (i.e., future intentions to volunteer, past volunteer experiences). While the research team tried to ensure that participants had completed at least ten hours of community service, four of the probationers who had just started their community service and had little to say about the experience were inadvertently referred to us by the probation office. We include their responses in the analysis because they also answered questions about their attitudes toward community service as a punishment. All interviews were recorded and transcribed.

2.4 Qualitative Coding and Analysis

The data were coded using Atlas.ti. The research team used a two-cycle coding technique to analyze the data (Miles et al., 2020; Saldaña, 2016). The first cycle involved descriptive coding, where the main topic of each passage was coded as a word or phrase. The second cycle involved pattern coding, where similar descriptive codes were grouped together into patterns or themes. We report these themes with supportive quotes from the study participants.

The interviews with the probationers included some quantitative questions. These questions asked the respondents to indicate how strongly they agreed with a given statement, using the following scale: (1) strongly disagree, (2) somewhat disagree, (3) neutral, (4) somewhat agree, and (5) strongly agree. When interviewees disagreed with one of the statements, they were asked to elaborate on why they selected that response. The statements read to the CSWs included: The probation office gave me choices in community service assignment, and my community service assignment is fair. We analyzed these questions by determining the percent of CSWs who agreed or strongly agreed with the statement.

3 Study Participants

This section provides background information on the research participants. We start with a brief description of the organizations in our study, including their primary mission area and how long they have worked with CSWs. Next, we describe the professional background, volunteer management knowledge, and experience of the managers responsible for overseeing the CSWs at those organizations. Finally, we provide a descriptive overview of the CSWs who were interviewed as part of this study.

3.1 Which Organizations Use Community Service Workers?

Many different types of organizations use CSWs. Twenty-five of our volunteer manager respondents work for nonprofit organizations (two work for the same nonprofit), and six work for public agencies. These organizations represent a range of purposes and mission areas. Nine are human service organizations, providing a range of direct services to individuals and families. Five are thrift stores. Four organizations operate in the area of sports and recreation. Three are health/medical organizations. Another three organizations focus on animal welfare. Two organizations focus on education and literacy. The remaining four organizations represent a range of mission areas – religious, membership-based, arts and culture, and human rights.

Most of the organizations in our study have a long history of working with CSWs. Five organizations reported working with CSWs for more than twenty years, and six reported working with CSWs for more than ten years. However, several interviewees did not know how long the organization had been working with CSWs because it predated their employment. Only a couple of organizations had started working with CSWs during the last year or two. Interestingly, four organizations reported that they have worked with CSWs "on and off." One respondent explained that their hiatus from working with CSWs was due to building renovations. A couple of organizations only use CSWs to help with a large (typically yearly) event. Overall, the responding organizations had been working with CSWs for many years. The number of CSWs at each organization also varied greatly. Some organizations only work with one or two CSWs a month. Other organizations use dozens of CSWs, particularly thrift stores and animal organizations. Our sample of organizations exhibited considerable variation in the number of CSWs at their site.

3.2 Who Are the Volunteer Managers?

When conducting our interviews, we asked to speak with the employee (or board member) at the organization with responsibility for overseeing CSWs. Where this responsibility was assigned varied greatly by organization. Table 1 shows some basic background information on the volunteer managers in our sample. Only five respondents have the job title of "volunteer coordinator" or "volunteer manager." Our sample included a few executive directors or assistant executive directors, and the bulk of the remaining respondents had some other managerial or supervisory role in the organization (e.g., store manager, facilities manager, case manager). A few respondents held positions on the organization's board, such as the president or secretary. No matter the job title, all of our respondents were responsible for overseeing both CSWs and volunteers. We, therefore, refer to our respondents as "volunteer managers" or "managers" throughout, despite the variation in their actual job titles.

The volunteer managers exhibited a wide range of backgrounds and experience. About two-thirds of our respondents had spent their entire careers in the nonprofit sector. Five had been employed previously in the business sector, and five had spent some time working for different public agencies. On average, respondents had worked at their current organization for nine years. Six respondents had been with their organization for two years or less, and four

Table 1 Volunteer managers' background information

Pseudonym	Org. name	Type	Position	Total work experience (years)	Total experience in the current organization (years)	Percent Time Managing Vols/CSWs	Background
Liam	Thrift Store	Nonprofit	Store Manager	30	1.4	No response	Business (Investment)
Olivia	Thrift Store	Nonprofit	Store Manager	Not asked	4	15	Nonprofit
Emma	Thrift Store	Nonprofit	Outreach Coordinator	0.4	0.4	25	First-time employee
Noah	Religious Organization	Nonprofit	Facilities Manager	4	4	13	Nonprofit
Amelia	Membership Association	Nonprofit	Board Secretary (Volunteer Position)	26	10	No response	Private probation
Oliver	Human Services	Nonprofit	Facilities Manager	1.5	1.5	10	First-time employee
Ava	Health/Medical	Nonprofit	Principal Manager	37	35	5	Nonprofit
Elijah	Education/ Literacy	Public	Volunteer Coordinator	30	30	25	Public Organization (library)
Sophia	Sports/Recreation	Nonprofit	Volunteer Manager (Volunteer Position)	30	0 (Volunteer)	25	Management
Isabella	Health/Medical	Nonprofit	Events & Communications Coordinator	15	4	30	Nonprofit
Luna	Human Services	Nonprofit	Assistant Director	2	2	10	First-time employee
Mia	Human Services	Nonprofit	Executive Coordinator	25	5	30	Business (Banking)
Charlotte	Animal Welfare	Nonprofit	Director	10	10	10	Nonprofit

Name	Cause Area	Sector	Title				
Mateo	Animal Welfare	Nonprofit	Director	Not asked	4	8	Nonprofit
Lucas	Human Services	Nonprofit	Volunteer Manager	15	5	45	Nonprofit
Evelyn	Sports/Recreation	Public	Parks Manager	Some	2.5	10	Public Organization
Levi	Human Rights	Nonprofit	Director	12	8	10	Nonprofit
Harper	Sports/Recreation	Public	Assistant Director	Some	15	40	Nonprofit
Scarlett	Thrift Store	Nonprofit	Store Manager	12	12	13	Nonprofit
Nova	Thrift Store	Nonprofit	Volunteer Coordinator	1.5	1.5	43	First-time employee
Asher	Education/ Literacy	Nonprofit	Program Manager	1.5	1.5	34	First-time employee
Aurora	Human Services	Public	Communications Director & Property Manager	Some	7	5	Nonprofit
James	Arts & Culture	Public	Security Manager	21.5	1.5	15	Public Organization (law enforcement)
Ella	Health/Medical	Nonprofit	Executive Director	Some	18	18	Public Organization (Navy)
Leo	Animal Welfare	Public	Animal Control Supervisor	Some	21	5	Nonprofit
Mila	Human Services	Nonprofit	Service Director & Case Manager	Some	3.5	8	Nonprofit
Aria	Human Services	Nonprofit	Director of Development & Volunteer Services	Some	2.5	13	Public Organization (State Park)
Ellie	Human Services	Nonprofit	Director	5	5	10	First-time employee
Gianna	Sports/Recreation	Nonprofit	Assistant Director	26	26	20	Nonprofit
Sofia	Thrift Store	Nonprofit	Thrift Center Manager	Not asked	8	28	Small Business
Grayson	Human Services	Nonprofit	Kitchen Manager	Not asked	8	85	Small Business & Nonprofit

reported working for the same organization for twenty or more years. Our sample thus represents a broad set of perspectives on the organization's work and the involvement of CSWs.

Most of our respondents had wider job responsibilities than just volunteer management. The five interviewees with the title of "volunteer manager/coordinator" tended to spend more time on volunteer management activities as a percent of their job (ranging from 25 to 45 percent of their time) than did the other respondents. Seventeen respondents indicated that volunteer management activities were 20 percent or less of their total work time. One respondent reported that volunteer management activities comprise 85 percent of his job, and three other respondents said that volunteer management took between 40 and 50 percent of their time. This means that all of our respondents had to balance volunteer management tasks with other roles and responsibilities, and most spent only a small proportion of their time on overall volunteer management, including CSW management.

3.2.1 Background in Volunteer Management

The volunteer managers also varied greatly in the amount of volunteer management training and professional development they received. One manager had received a certificate for volunteer services from the Georgia Department of Community Health, and another manager had achieved a volunteer management credential through a parent organization. None of the other respondents had received any specific credentials related to volunteer management, including certifications offered outside their organizations' auspices, such as the Certification in Volunteer Administration.[1] When asked about credentialing, several volunteer managers stated that they had other educational accomplishments that touched on volunteer management, such as a Master of Social Work, a Master of Public Administration, or a graduate certificate in Nonprofit Management & Leadership.

Several volunteer managers expressed their belief that managing volunteers does not require any specialized skills beyond general management. A quote from one volunteer manager, Aurora, sums up the feelings of these respondents: "Managing a volunteer isn't much different from managing an actual staff member. You treat everyone respectfully. You try to find out what their set of skills is. You find out if something is not going well, you can try and correct it in the beginning, so you can have a relationship going forward that works (Aurora)." Several respondents had a lot of general management experience and believed that this experience and training were sufficient to enable them to manage volunteers effectively.

---

[1] The Certification in Volunteer Administration is a competency-based certification program for volunteer manager sponsored by the Council for Certification in Volunteer Administration. https://cvacert.org/

There was a great deal of variation in the managers' management-related professional development. Seven managers reported that they had not received any professional development to enhance their skills as volunteer managers in the past three years. As one manager, Charlotte, put it, "I really haven't had any [professional development]. It's really been trial by fire." Another seven respondents indicated that the only training they received regarding volunteer management was the required training offered through the probation office (which we describe in the next section). The remaining respondents had participated in a range of relevant professional development activities, including courses through a parent organization, courses through infrastructure organizations or other nonprofits (e.g., Chamber of Commerce, Nonprofit Resource Center), university or continuing education courses, related specialized training (e.g., conflict resolution, general management), or training provided by their organization.

When the managers were unsure how best to manage volunteers, they tended to depend on their own experiences or advice from a supervisor, other colleagues at the organization, or their peer networks. A few respondents reported that if they had a question or problem with CSWs, they would reach out to the local probation office. Some respondents indicated that they sought answers by referring to their organizations' policies or procedures. Beyond that, very few managers would actively seek best practices in volunteer management or related information to help them with their work. The few who did would mostly consult websites or popular management books for advice. One manager, Nova, explained why these managers invest so little in professional development:

> I am not actively seeking information. We are kind of in a rut right now on how we do volunteer coordination, and I'm not trying to get out of that yet. We've found a system that works with us, and honestly, since the volunteer coordination position is not a sole position, it's just something I do, I don't have time to train myself or look for more knowledge about volunteer coordination. (Nova)

Given that volunteer management is a small proportion of their work tasks, these managers lack incentives to invest time in researching better processes and procedures.

3.3 Who Are the Court-Ordered Community Service Workers?

The research team also conducted interviews with thirty-four individuals on probation who have community service requirements. Of these thirty-four CSWs, eighteen were supervised by the Dogwood Office and fourteen by the Azalea Office. Table 2 depicts basic demographic information for the CSWs in our study. Fifteen of the CSWs were female (44 percent). The CSWs also tended

Table 2 Community service workers' demographic and probation information

Pseudonym	Gender	Race	Age (as of 2018)	Employment	Education	Household income	Offense	Total probation period (months)	Completed hours/ total community service (hours)
Ezra	Male	White	38	40 or more hours a week	Some college	$20,001–$40,000	Vehicular crimes	12	40/40
Violet	Female	White	N/A	40 or more hours a week	Some college	$20,001–$40,000	Theft	12	30/80
Luca	Male	White	32	40 or more hours a week	Bachelor's degree	$40,001–$60,000	Vehicular crimes	12	15/40
Ethan	Male	White	62	Unemployed	Bachelor's degree	$20,001–$40,000	Vehicular crimes/theft	12	330/330
Aden	Male	White	45	Unemployed	High school/GED	Up to $20,000	Vehicular crimes	36	144/240
Layla	Female	White	20	20–28 hours a week	Some college	Up to $20,000	Vehicular crimes/ underage drinking	12	120/120
Wyatt	Male	White	20	Less than 20 hours a week	Some college	Up to $20,000	Underage drinking	12	40/40
Willow	Female	Hispanic	25	Unemployed	Less than high school	Up to $20,000	Theft by receiving	12	40/40
Lily	Female	White	46	40 or more hours a week	Some college	Up to $20,000	Traffic ticket	6	11/30
Sebastian	Male	White	19	Less than 20 hours a week	High school/GED	More than $120,000	Fake ID/underage drinking	12	22/40
Hazel	Female	White	29	20–28 hours a week	Bachelor's degree	$20,001–$40,000	Theft by taking	10	100/160
Camila	Female	White	19	40 or more hours a week	High school/GED	$20,001–$40,000	Theft	6	20/40
Benjamin	Male	White	22	40 or more hours a week	Less than high school	$40,000–$60,000	Drug offenses/ underage drinking	12	10/80
Avery	Female	Other	18	30–39 hours a week	High school/GED	$20,001–$40,000	Theft	6	30/40

Name	Gender	Race	Age	Employment	Education	Income	Offense		
Mason	Male	Black	36	Unemployed	High school/GED	Up to $20,000	Drug offenses	12	12/40
Chloe	Female	White	20	Unemployed	Some college	$100,001–$12,000	Fake ID/underage Drinking	12	24/60
Henry	Male	White	32	Unemployed	Bachelor's degree	$20,001–$40,000	Vehicular crimes	12	30/40
Hudson	Male	Black	23	Less than 20 hours a week	Some college	Up to $20,000	Drug offenses	12	31/120
Jack	Male	Other	20	Unemployed	Some college	More than $120,000	Underage drinking	12	30/30
Jackson	Male	White	19	20–28 hours a week	High school/GED	$20,001–$40,000	Vehicular crimes/underage alcohol possession	36	130/130
Elena	Female	White	30	20–28 hours a week	High school/GED	Up to $20,000	Theft	60+	0/40
Owen	Male	Black	40	40 or more hours a week	High school/GED	$20,001–$40,000	Drug offenses	60+	0/50
Daniel	Male	Hispanic	25	40 or more hours a week	High school/GED	$100,000–$120,000	Vehicular crimes/drug offenses	60	6/120
Paisley	Female	White	28	Unemployed	High school/GED	Up to $20,000	Theft	60	3/40
Eliana	Female	White	36	Unemployed	Some college	$60,000–$80,000	Theft/drug offenses	60+	6/40
Alexander	Male	White	36	40 or more hours a week	Some college	$20,001–$40,000	Drug offenses	60+	34/40
Maverick	Male	White	50	40 or more hours a week	High school/GED	Up to $20,000	Property crimes	60+	0/20
Penelope	Female	White	21	20–28 hours a week	Less than high school	Up to $20,000	Theft	36	26.5/40
Eleanor	Female	White	49	Unemployed	High school/GED	Up to $20,000	Drug offenses	48	11/40
Ivy	Female	White	29	Unemployed	Some college	Up to $20,000	Theft	60+	0/40
Kai	Male	White	42	Unemployed	High school/GED	Up to $20,000	Other (family violence)	60	20/20

Table 2 (cont.)

Pseudonym	Gender	Race	Age (as of 2018)	Employment	Education	Household income	Offense	Total probation period (months)	Completed hours/ total community service (hours)
Gabriel	Male	White	58	40 or more hours a week	High school/GED	$40,000–$60,000	Vehicular crimes/drug offenses	48	5/40
Elizabeth	Female	White	32	30–39 hours a week	High School/GED	Up to $20,000	Drug	60+	4/40
Carter	Male	White	21	40 or more hours a week	Less than high school	$20,001–$40,000	Vehicular crimes/ violent crimes/ theft/disorderly conduct	60	29/40

to be white (twenty-seven out of thirty-four) and young (seventeen are under age thirty). Only four CSWs held a bachelor's degree, although eleven had completed some college credit. The CSWs in our sample also tended to be from lower socioeconomic groups; twenty-six reported making $40,000 or less a year. They were pretty evenly split between being unemployed (twelve), employed part-time (ten), and employed full-time (twelve). Our sample includes seven college students.

Most of the CSWs reported that their probation term was a year or less (eighteen), but eleven CSWs were on probation for a term of five or more years. The CSWs were convicted of a variety of offenses, including vehicular crimes (21 percent; e.g., DUI, reckless driving, speeding); drug offenses (15 percent; e.g., possession of narcotics or other controlled substance offenses); underage drinking (26 percent); larceny (32 percent); and violent crimes (6 percent; e.g., assault).

The community service requirement varied greatly within the group. The total required community service hours ranged from 20 to 330 hours, with an average of 66 hours. On average, the CSW respondents had completed forty hours of community service at the time of the interviews. The CSWs fulfill their community service hours in a variety of public and nonprofit organizations. In our sample, sixteen CSWs worked in nonprofit organizations, such as thrift stores, animal shelters, and human service agencies. Another thirteen CSWs worked in public organizations, such as libraries or parks. Finally, three CSWs did their community service hours at local churches. Interestingly, the remaining two CSWs were disabled persons, so they were assigned by the probation office to pick up garbage in the neighborhood around the probation office for their community service hours. Several CSWs in our sample conducted their community service at organizations whose volunteer manager was interviewed as part of this study; however, several other CSWs performed community service at organizations that were not on the provided lists, so there is only a partial overlap between our sample of volunteer managers/organizations and our sample of CSWs.

4 Preparing for Community Service Workers

The first phase of our framework is preparing the organization to receive CSWs. We start by discussing the organization's rationales for bringing CSWs into the organization. This is followed by a description of the relationship the organizations have with the probation office, including the probation office's rules and regulations. Next, we consider the work/jobs that organizations design for CSWs and CSWs' perspectives on those tasks. Finally, we discuss the policies these organizations have developed for working with CSWs, especially policies around accepted offenses and open identification.

4.1 Why Organizations Use Community Service Workers

We asked the managers why their organization chose to work with CSWs. We learned that organizations work with CSWs for three main reasons – CSWs are a free and needed human resource, working with CSWs fits the organization's mission, and it increases their involvement in the community.

4.1.1 Free Human Resource

Most of the organizations reported that the decision to accept CSWs was due to their need for free human resources. The managers indicated that they "needed more manpower" (Amelia), "need the help" (Elijah), or "needed some muscle" (Ella), or that they just wanted the "free labor" (Liam, Noah, and Harper). Several organizations commented on their small staff size and the need for CSWs in order to increase the amount of work they could accomplish. One manager, Sofia, reported, "We are only allowed a limited number of staff on the site, so without CSWs, we couldn't get a lot of stuff done. We really expect them to come. They help us to keep the store going" (Sofia). Respondents viewed CSWs as helping them to get the organization's work done.

Beyond the need for labor in general, the managers indicated that CSWs were valuable because they are mandated to do a specific number of service hours, and there are consequences if they do not complete the hours. As one manager said: "We love regular volunteers, but having court-ordered CSWs . . . They have to be there. We can schedule them in advance. That's a big blessing to us" (Emma). Lucas stated, "there's more of a set schedule you can do, so you can expect them at certain times. Whereas some volunteers, you can set up a schedule, and there's no consequence for them if they don't show up. Whereas the community service worker, there's a little bit more of a consequence for them to show up." These responses indicate that CSWs were more helpful than volunteers because organizations can put them on a consistent work schedule and CSWs have an extra incentive to show up for their assignments.

One manager also appreciated the experience and skills that CSWs bring to the organization. "Since a lot of the CSWs, in their regular jobs, worked for companies like landscapers or construction, they had the best background to do anything we needed related to building maintenance or repairs" (Ellie). The respondent went on to say that the organization's young college student volunteers, in contrast, often didn't have relevant skillsets, so the manager would have to show them how to accomplish a maintenance-related task.

4.1.2 Mission-Related

Not only do CSWs provide needed labor, but working with CSWs fits with the broader mission of many of the organizations in our study. As one manager stated: "It's very much on mission for us to be able to provide a second chance opportunity for people in the community. It's kind of overlaps into what we want to do" (Emma). Lucas indicated:

> We had a lot of people who came to stay in our shelters who also had community service, so we thought we would help them along with that, get rid of their community service hours at the same time as getting shelter, housing, things like that. We noticed other people in the community needed that service as well. We decided to help with that. (Lucas)

For these managers, CSWs were either part of their clientele or they viewed them as an extension of their clientele – another group of people who could benefit from the organization.

Additionally, the managers wanted to teach the CSWs helpful life skills. As one manager stated:

> Our organization deals with communities that are disenfranchised, so because of our compassion of that clientele that overlaps into our volunteer-seeking individuals. We appreciate the person who is actively seeking employment and needs those soft skills. This is a great place to learn those soft skills. I'm guessing there are people that are court-ordered that need those developed, so that's why we want to open our doors to any volunteer that's willing to work with us. (Luna)

A second manager indicated that the organization hoped to teach individuals to be more responsible, especially as it relates to their mission. "Sometimes we have offenders who are in animal control violations, so we use it kind of like a teaching and learning experience for them on responsible ownership of pets" (Charlotte). Clearly, these managers hoped to influence the CSWs' lives by providing a setting where they could learn things that would benefit them as employees or community members.

4.1.3 Community-Related

Other volunteer managers mentioned general community benefits as a rationale for working with CSWs. In the words of one manager: "I guess it's just [our organization] figures it's our way of giving back to the community. There's not a lot of places to do community service" (Olivia). Another manager expressed an interest in just being an open place where anyone from the community could participate. "Well, we are definitely community open, and we want to accommodate anyone who wants to assist us in any way we can" (Levi). These responses indicate that these managers see their organizations as part of a larger community, and they want to be seen as welcoming.

Additionally, a few managers mentioned the reputational benefits of working with CSWs. They would "get the benefit of name recognition" (Isabella) and felt that "it does get us a lot more publicity, outreach into the community" (Mateo). One manager even mentioned it as an opportunity for people in the community to learn more about the organization and what it does (Aurora). These volunteer managers viewed working with CSWs as a way to build positive relationships with the community and to reach new audiences. "The only thing I can think of is it helps our stance with the community agency we are working with. If it's [Dogwood Office's] county police department or the sheriff's office, it helps show our community spirit certainly. . . . But, we do it because we want to be a good steward and be a good co-agency in the community" (Aria). For these organizations, working with CSWs helps them to contribute positively to their community.

4.2 Relationship with the Probation Office

No matter why an organization chooses to work with CSWs, they must develop a relationship with a probation office in order to receive CSWs. Community organizations have to follow the probation office's rules and regulations regarding CSWs, so it is important to understand these rules and how they are communicated. The two probation offices in our study have very different approaches.

4.2.1 Probation Office Rules and Regulations

The Dogwood Office has a vetting and training process for organizations that desire to use CSWs. Specifically, the organization must complete a mandatory training session, sign a Memorandum of Agreement, and provide a copy of their 501(c)3 designation from the IRS. The required training covers the Dogwood Office's rules for CSWs and the requirements that each participating organization must meet. The training also addresses the sanctions for CSWs and their supervisors who do not comply with the outlined policies. As part of the required training, representatives from each organization receive a handbook that describes the roles and responsibilities of each party – probation office, organization/supervisors, and CSWs – and examples of required documentation.

One important policy concerns timekeeping. Specifically, CSWs associated with the Dogwood Office are not allowed to handle their timekeeping document. As is commonly the case with organizational policies, this policy was developed in response to a problem, as suggested in what follows.

So we went to a meeting, and [the probation office] said not to even give [the CSWs] the form. Once they finish, mail them in. They'll call and verify. They had a group of people who were falsifying hours, and they got caught. The community service worker had 125 hours, and they had to start them hours over. And the girl who falsified them had to go to jail for one day for each hour they had. I wouldn't dare do that because you'd be in some big trouble. (Grayson)

Additionally, supervisors are instructed not to allow proxy community service for a CSW, accept money or gifts from CSWs, or even credit a lunch break as community service time. The Dogwood Office instituted these rules because they had issues in the past with CSWs bribing supervisors to sign off on community service hours they had not performed. The Dogwood Office also asks to be kept informed about which individual is serving as their primary contact with the organization and the organization's work locations and hours of operation.

Interestingly, the Dogwood Office also requires organizations to identify CSWs as community service workers to the organizations' staff, volunteers, and clients. That identification typically involves some type of visual marker, such as a vest or t-shirt, that must be worn at all times while doing community service.

The Dogwood Office also provides guidance on the type of work CSWs should perform. "The type of work typically involves neighborhood clean-up, janitorial services, landscaping, maintenance, skilled labor, and clerical work. The needs and safety of the community and the organization, as well as the skills of the probationer, are taken into consideration when making placements" (Anonymized Probation Office, 2018). While discretion is given to individual organizations, they are encouraged to engage CSWs in manual labor of some kind. Community service workers are not allowed to have cell phones during community service hours except in case of emergency.

In addition, the Dogwood Office trains CSWs regarding the fulfillment of their service hours. They are required to read and sign a copy of the rules for CSWs and to sign a waiver of liability form. Community service workers are coached on appropriate behavior, such as not bringing drugs, alcohol, or weapons to their service site and interacting appropriately with other individuals.

In contrast to the Dogwood Office, the Azalea Office does not provide any formal training for partner organizations or a formal process for setting expectations for CSWs. The Azalea Office also has different rules and procedures for supervising CSWs. For example, the Azalea Office typically has CSWs perform their first ten community service hours at their office location so that the officers can assess their level of cooperation and compliance. Essentially, they prescreen CSWs before sending them out to work in community organizations. The Azalea Office experiences a high level of noncompliance with community service requirements, and they are mindful of the burden this can place on their partner organizations.

The Azalea Office is very sensitive to the needs of individual CSWs and the obstacles they face in doing community service. For example, the Azalea Office allows those with mental or physical disabilities to perform alternative services, such as picking up garbage. Additionally, the Azalea Office has a smaller number of partner organizations receiving CSWs than the Dogwood Office, and those organizations are spread across several rural counties. As a result, it is very challenging for CSWs attached to the Azalea Office to complete their service hours, especially those without reliable transportation, because they must often travel far to their service site. Fewer potential community service sites can also make it more difficult for CSWs to schedule community service around work and family commitments. These substantial barriers to compliance are reflected in the Azalea Office's flexibility in working with CSWs.

Several of the community agencies in our study, however, also supervised CSWs from other probation offices. Sometimes, their CSWs were on probation in one jurisdiction but received permission to do their service in another jurisdiction because they temporarily reside there (i.e., college students). None of the managers received any training or guidance from the probation offices in these other counties. In fact, they rarely had any contact with these other offices because they permitted CSWs to handle their own time logs. Respondents particularly singled out private probation offices as lacking rules and regulations: "No, I'm going to say that unfortunately so many of the private probation companies seem to be winging it . . . I don't know what their policies are. The governmental agencies tend to have some very specific requirements, whereas the private companies I have not seen that level of precision" (Elijah). It is very interesting how little regulation and oversight most probation offices provide for community service, particularly regarding timekeeping.

We found that volunteer managers appreciated the rules and procedures provided by the Dogwood Office, as it provided structure for the community service program. As Ellie stated:

> I rely a lot on the information from the [Dogwood Office] because they have what seems to me to be the best developed program. Best set-up, structure, rules, and the clearest communication of what they expect. Those seem to be the best thought out, the most organized . . . The other offices I've dealt with, honestly, it seems like they just give them a list of sites and push them out the door.

Several managers indicated that they use the Dogwood Office rules and proced-ures for all CSWs regardless of the probation office that sent them because the Dogwood Office rules made sense and helped their work with CSWs to go more smoothly. "We think that [the Dogwood Office] has the best policies. They did the most recent revamp of their program and have . . . It's up to the standard we like to keep. So, the rules they give us, we just apply to every worker. Just to keep it consistent but also because their practices are generally the best practices" (Emma). Clearly, there is wide variation in how different counties handle community service, including the level of oversight provided and the procedures and rules for working with CSWs. It also seemed that the managers in our study appreciated having more instruction, guidance, and support in working with CSWs.

4.2.2 Lessons Learned about Interactions with the Probation Office

Probation offices have a great deal of influence over how well court-ordered community service works, yet there is wide variation in how they implement community service. The two probation offices in our sample had contrasting approaches to managing community service. The Dogwood Office was unusually professional and proactive in its approach to community service, while the Azalea Office used a more flexible and accommodating approach. Our analysis hints at some important factors that affect how a probation office administers community service, such as the size of the geographic area served, the availability of public transportation, the number of community organizations willing to work with CSWs, and the abilities of the CSWs themselves (e.g., people with physical or mental disabilities).

Private probation offices were particularly challenging to work with. Though all of the CSWs in our study reported to either the Dogwood or Azalea probation offices, both of which were state-run agencies, some managers in our study had experience managing CSWs who reported to private probation companies. These managers reported negative experiences with private probation companies, citing a lack of guidance and oversight. This is consistent with research findings that the private probation industry is poorly regulated, and because of its profit motive, it is disinclined to spend money on programs that would improve the probation experience, such as officer training (Huebner & Shannon, 2022).

Our results indicate that the managers preferred working with probation offices that provided them with clear policies and direction, such as the support and structure they received from the Dogwood Office. Consistent with prior research (Allen & Treger, 1990), we find that many community agencies desire greater communication from the probation office. Given the paucity of research regarding the management of CSWs and the limited practitioner advice on the subject, community organizations relied on the probation offices to help them develop effective policies. In particular, community organizations desire that probation offices: communicate more effectively, train probationers on how to do community service, provide easy reporting procedures, help screen out difficult CSWs, and provide general advice and support (Allen & Treger, 1990; McIvor, 1993a).

We suspect that the amount and type of support from probation offices affect the willingness of community organizations to receive CSWs – something that can be investigated in future research. Community organizations that have negative experiences with CSWs may discontinue working with them, further limiting opportunities for placement. A supportive probation office – especially one that provides training and screening for CSWs – can enable more community organizations to work with CSWs by helping to prevent and manage problems. Additionally, the probation office's actions might also affect CSWs' willingness to participate in community service and their success at completing their hours. For example, probation offices that have outdated lists of organizations willing to receive CSWs or that provide little support to CSWs in finding placements might have lower compliance with community service requirements.

4.3 Community Service Workers' Tasks

As shown in our framework, another important component of preparing to work with CSWs is planning out what work they will do within the organization. The managers described which tasks CSWs were permitted to perform at their organizations. Per the guidance from the Dogwood Office, most organizations primarily used CSWs for manual labor – general cleaning, lawn maintenance, and moving items. In several organizations, CSWs participated in event setup/take-down and served as "gophers" during an event. Depending on the organization's services and needs, CSWs would do manual labor more specifically related to that organization. For example, in thrift stores, CSWs would accept and sort donations, stock shelves, and load/unload large items.

Several managers pointed out that CSWs would do the same types of tasks as their volunteers. Typically, when volunteers were permitted to do something that CSWs were not permitted to do, it was because those volunteers had been around longer, knew organization policies and procedures better, or had been trained to do a particular task. For example, the animal-related organizations limited CSWs' interactions with animals because they did not know how experienced they were with animals and they wanted to avoid animal bites and scratches. But generally speaking, the volunteer managers saw little distinction between tasks performed by CSWs and those performed by their volunteers.

There were certain common tasks, though, that organizations would typically not permit CSWs to perform. None of the organizations would permit the CSWs to handle money or work on a cash register, except for one organization that allowed CSWs to swipe credit cards at an event under staff supervision. None of the organizations would permit CSWs to do anything related to alcohol. Most of the managers specifically indicated that they did not allow CSWs to perform tasks that would give them access to individuals' private information. In addition, few CSWs interacted with clients, and when they did, it was typically a brief, casual encounter, such as answering a phone, staffing a sign-in booth at an event, or helping customers in a thrift store or food bank. Some organizations had prohibitions on activities that might be dangerous (e.g., going on the roof) or required additional training (e.g., operating heavy machinery).

Some enterprising managers sought to understand CSWs' skills and interests and use those as a basis for their work assignments. "If they have a specific skill, we will use that" (Evelyn), said one volunteer manager. Another manager described her process by saying: "We have also had people … that helped us with organizing the files. Then another one … said she was good at organizing things, so I turned her loose on our supply closet. We have another person now who's helping with our English class because he's bilingual and he's really good at teaching" (Ellie). Overall, the needs of the organization dictated the tasks assigned to CSWs, but when possible, several organizations tried to be creative in fitting CSWs' tasks to their skills.

4.3.1 Community Service Workers' Perspectives on Their Tasks

We asked CSWs what type of labor they performed at the organization, and their responses mirrored the managers' reports. Community service workers did manual labor (e.g., loading and unloading donations, landscape work, construction), janitorial service (e.g., cleaning, mopping, sweeping, dishwashing, laundry), and clerical work (e.g., note taking, filing documents, keeping an inventory of supplies). Community service workers reported that they were not allowed to do certain tasks, such as handling money. Community service workers were often excluded from direct service work, such as making contact with the clients of the organizations. In most cases, though, CSWs were assigned tasks based on the organization's daily needs, such as cleaning, sorting donations, and other manual work, rather than regularly performed or scheduled tasks or responsibilities.

Unlike regular volunteers, CSWs are required to work for a specific number of hours – sometimes over 300 or more hours. This gave the staff time to get to know the CSWs and learn to trust them. For example, Ethan, who worked reliably in a thrift store for more than 300 hours, ended up being in charge of all tasks in the store, including sorting valuables and money-related tasks that were generally prohibited for CSWs. So, the amount of time a CSW has put in, their personal reliability, and work quality can lead organizations to give them more complex tasks or those involving more responsibility.

Many CSWs showed total indifference to the tasks they performed, regardless of how many service hours they were assigned. They expected that the tasks given to them would be either trivial or difficult and would be work that the staff or other general volunteers did not have time for or did not want to do. As one CSW, Lily, reported, "You just do tons of odd things they don't have anybody else to do. . . . I have just started to do what they ask me to do. So, I haven't asked an extra question or anything." CSWs did not express their preferences or register complaints about given tasks; they typically just complied. As another CSW said, "There is a list that we go off for, so I don't do others than outside the list. I don't ask to do anything that is not permitted" (Gabriel).

While there was a high level of compliance with the tasks they were assigned, some CSWs noticed that their tasks were limited. One CSW said, "I guess there was a lot of stuff that was going on that I wasn't allowed to do" (Wyatt). Another CSW who had done community service at multiple organizations indicated:

> In one of the animal shelters and it says that people who are on probation will have absolutely no contact with the animals. So, it's like immediately written on the sheet. In some organizations, you do only janitorial work or something like that. . . . There were certain things like immediately you could or couldn't do. It was immediately laid out for you. (Henry)

We asked CSWs which types of tasks they would like to do that they are not permitted to do, and they indicated that they wanted to engage with more people (especially the clients of the organization) (Layla and Avery) and have opportunities to understand the organizational operations and management (Hazel and Henry).

4.3.2 Community Service Workers' Interactions with Clients

Despite limitations on their tasks, some CSWs also reported a rewarding experience with the clients at the organization. Six CSWs had the opportunity to interact with and help a client, and that experience made a strong impression on them. Typically, these types of experiences involved helping clients in a public environment, like finding clothing or items in a thrift store or preparing and serving food at a soup kitchen. One CSW, Aden, especially enjoyed his client interactions:

> Helping this lady who had a child, and they were homeless. Helping her with clothing for her child, food, general information for assistance, that type of thing. It was just really nice to do something nice for someone and they genuinely appreciated it. And also, a child being involved, that also, as me

being a father, that was very important and ensured that the child was getting clothing, food, assistance, and everything was. You know . . . that child looked happy, and it didn't look like the child was being harmed or anything. That . . . that was a very positive experience for me.

It was very interesting that even one meaningful interaction with an organization's clients could be the most memorable positive experience for a CSW. Violet spent more than 400 hours doing community service in a variety of organizations. Her tasks at all these organizations varied from cleaning and manual work to feeding the homeless. Violet expressed great satisfaction with the opportunity to interact with the homeless clientele. She found it meaningful because she felt she had an impact on them. She described it this way, "From their eyes, I helped some . . . I can see it in her face that she really enjoyed it. She was very thankful for what I've done. . . . I realized that there are actually people in the world that do need help." Few CSWs in our sample were permitted to have any interaction with clients, and those that did had limited opportunities to do so. However, when CSWs did have those opportunities, they tended to be positive and memorable.

4.3.3 Lessons Learned about Creating Meaningful Work for Community Service Workers

Today's volunteers are very demanding and want to do high-quality jobs – work that they find meaningful and impactful (Dwyer et al., 2013; Kulik, 2006). Volunteers typically prefer not to do simple, menial tasks; they enjoy challenge and variety (Hobson, 2007; Jamison, 2003; Van Schie et al., 2015). Yet, menial tasks typically get passed on to CSWs. Prior research also substantiates the fact that CSWs tend to perform manual labor (McIvor, 1993a, 1993b). The nature of court-mandated community service results in CSWs doing work that most people would not find rewarding. This could be another missed opportunity. As long as CSWs only perform menial tasks, the potential for community service to change their lives is limited since the work will be seen as merely a punishment that does not contribute to a broader community goal. As Bazemore and Karp (2004, p. 20) state: "community service activity that is clearly directed toward meeting the needs of the less fortunate or young people will be more likely to change the role and self-image of formerly incarcerated persons than work which is perceived as irrelevant or punitive."

While most CSWs in our sample were not permitted to work directly with clients, a few CSWs experienced some client interactions, such as serving food to the homeless. Community service workers described those as meaningful experiences. They tended to cite these experiences as among the most meaningful or positive experiences they had while doing their community service. This finding fits well with empirical studies that find positive effects of meaningful tasks on volunteer satisfaction and retention (Finkelstein, 2008; Hidalgo & Moreno, 2009; Stukas et al., 2009; Van Schie et al., 2015). Perhaps community service would have a more powerful impact on CSWs' attitudes, behaviors, and perspectives if it could be redesigned to include more meaningful work and client interactions. While we recognize organizations' concerns about risk management, it is likely that many organizations could provide more structured, supervised, appropriate interactions between clients and CSWs. Research on community service in Scotland revealed that almost half of the organizations allowed CSWs a great deal of contact with their clients (McIvor, 1993a), indicating that this can be successfully achieved. Positive client interactions can help CSWs feel that they are truly doing something to serve their communities and actually helping other people.

Good volunteer work design leads to greater satisfaction and intention to continue volunteering among volunteers (Hidalgo & Moreno, 2009; Kulik, 2006; Van Schie et al., 2015). Good work design could also lead to greater satisfaction and more positive outcomes for CSWs, such as continuing as a volunteer after their community service is complete. Prior research has shown that many organizations can retain CSWs as volunteers after their community service is complete (McIvor, 1993a) – a phenomenon that can benefit both the community organization and the CSW. We stress that community service will not be likely to achieve its goals without providing CSWs with more meaningful opportunities to contribute.

4.4 Policies about Community Service Workers

The last part of preparing to receive CSWs is developing policies to support the program. We asked the managers to describe their organization's policies for working with CSWs. Nine managers indicated that they had no special policies for CSWs beyond the Dogwood Office's policies. In fact, several managers emphasized that there was little to no difference between the rules for CSWs and the rules governing volunteers. "They follow the rules too. . . . The rules are for workers, community services, and everybody. We don't have any exceptions" (Scarlett). Sometimes, the only real difference between CSWs and other volunteers is a stricter timekeeping requirement. Yet in many organizations, all volunteers have to sign in when they come and sign out when they leave, so tracking hours is not unique to CSWs.

The managers, though, tended to be stricter with CSWs, such as enforcing a no cell phone policy and ensuring that CSWs are working rather than wasting time or socializing. One manager described it this way:

> We would not allow CSWs to hang around using their cell phones. Basically, they're here to work, and if they're not working, then they don't get to be here as opposed to volunteers, who they can hang out all day if they want to. And they can play with the dogs, or they can hang out in the kennel. I mean, we don't have any real specific requirements for volunteers. Does that make sense? (Leo)

The managers felt that CSWs were obligated to put in an hour of real work in order for it to count toward their community service hours, while they were more flexible and tolerant of volunteers.

Another major policy pertained to work scheduling and conditions for termination. Many organizations have a policy that CSWs need to call 24 hours in advance if they will miss a shift. They also have policies that after a certain number of "no-shows" (typically three), the CSW is terminated, and their records are sent back to the probation office. Two organizations also determined that any employee could terminate a belligerent or uncooperative CSW on the spot.

> After so many people had bad attitudes, we decided that any employee can dismiss a community service worker at any time. That doesn't have to be just a supervisor. If someone is just too difficult to work with, we have the right to not let them do community service with us. We have decided that any employee has the right to do that. (Olivia)

As that manager indicated, those policies were developed due to prior difficulties dealing with CSWs who were not following organization policies, doing their work, or using good communication and people skills.

The managers who described special policies pertaining to CSWs reported that those policies were developed in response to problems rather than in a search for best practices or previously designed management strategies. Emma described it this way: "I don't think that there was ever one moment where we sat down and revamped everything. I think as we ran into problems with individual workers, we decided to change different policies." An example of a policy set in response to a problem is one organization that stipulates that male CSWs are only allowed to work with male staff and female CSWs with female staff. Managers also adjusted policies as necessary to ensure a conducive working environment.

> So, with the phones, they would be on their phones and not working. So that was an incentive to get rid of the distraction. They can't speak to each other, and that came out of we had friends that would get arrested together and then come in and want to serve their community service together, and that would be a distraction. So, I guess a lot of the policies came out of minimizing distractions from their work. So, any policies we have in place would be to do that. (Mateo)

Organizational rules for CSWs, while sometimes reactive, were not very onerous and focused on having a productive and safe working environment. However, two sets of policies deserve special attention – accepted offenses and open identification.

4.4.1 Policies about Accepted Offenses

Typically, the decision about which offenses the organization would accept was up to the manager. None of the organizations in our sample would accept CSWs with a history of sexual crimes. All but two of the organizations would not accept probationers who had committed any type of violent crime. One exception is a faith-based human services organization where the volunteer manager said that receiving a violent offender "depends on what kind of attitude he comes in with" (Oliver). A few volunteer managers indicated that their organization would accept a CSW with a nonviolent felony charge on a case-by-case basis, but most would not. All of the organizations would accept traffic offenses, such as DUI, speeding, or reckless driving, as well as underage drinking. There was a great deal of variation in the acceptance of property crimes (e.g., theft, shoplifting) and drug-related charges (e.g., possession of controlled substances), although the majority of organizations would accept CSWs with those charges. Beyond violent and sexual crimes, most volunteer managers seemed fairly open to a variety of crimes. As one volunteer manager stated, "They just come rolling through the door, and we pretty much just take anybody" (Charlotte).

The rationale behind deciding which charges to accept typically centered on the working environment and the level of interaction with clients. One volunteer manager summed it up well by saying:

> Well, because of our environment, the CSWs aren't necessarily engaging with customers, but they are present in the near vicinity and can affect the customer experience. We wanted to make sure our customers and any kind of constituent would be aware they are in a safe environment. They didn't need to feel uncomfortable while they're with us. Also, we have about 12 store employees, and we want our employees to feel safe. They work hand-in-hand with the CSWs. . . . So, for that reason, we decided not to do any kind of violent crimes or felonies or anything like that. As far as shoplifting and trespassing, that's strictly just protecting ourselves, since it's a retail environment. We don't need to deal with people who are stealing merchandise. (Emma)

Several other managers made similar comments. Staff safety and comfort were important concerns, which is why few organizations accepted violent offenses and none would accept sexual offenses.

Client interaction was another factor affecting organizations' decisions about which charges to accept. While most CSWs did not perform tasks directly related to client interaction, they sometimes performed tasks in the vicinity of clients. In these environments, the managers were typically more strict in determining which offenses to accept. "Based on the fact that we interact with the public, and we feel like the folks, even those who work us behind the scenes and may never come in contact with the public, are still a reflection of the organization" (Elijah). In one instance, a volunteer manager indicated that her CSWs had no client interaction, so she was willing to accept anyone (outside of violent and sexual crimes) (Aria). In general, organizations were cautious about the level of interaction their CSWs would have with clients.

Organizations with retail operations, like thrift stores, tended not to accept individuals with theft charges. Acceptance of drug-related charges also depended on the working environment and clientele served. As one manager in a health-related organization said: "because of HIPPA, you don't want anybody who is a patient or connected to a patient. Because we have a pharmacy on-site and needles/syringes, you want to be very careful you don't take anybody who is a shoplifter or who uses drugs" (Ella). To a certain extent, the organization's mission and services shaped decisions about which CSWs to accept.

4.4.2 Community Service Workers' Perspectives on Accepted Offenses

Organizational policies limiting accepted offenses were problematic from the CSWs' perspectives. Community service workers already have relatively few options for community service, and this challenge is compounded by the fact that few organizations have evening or weekend service opportunities. The addition of screening based on offense made it very difficult for some CSWs to find workable placements. As Owen stated, "But because of my charges, I have drug offenses, so some places you can't do community service for them." Clear communication between the community organization and the probation office could alleviate some of this burden, as probation officers could then steer CSWs to organizations willing to accept their offenses. However, in some instances, CSWs did not find out until later in the process that they would not be accepted by a particular organization. "I was assigned a place originally, but that didn't work. I had to find a different place. Finding a place that was going to take someone with theft by receiving was hard because the moment you mentioned theft, they didn't want you" (Willow). CSWs with theft and drug charges were not accepted at every location, so they struggled more to find a placement than CSWs with traffic offenses. Community service workers with violent offenses had the hardest time of all because very few organizations were willing to accept those charges. This indicates a mismatch between what criminal offenses community organizations will accept and which individuals are sentenced to community service.

4.4.3 Policies about Open Identification of Community Service Workers

Another relevant policy pertains to openly identifying CSWs within the organization. We asked the managers whether the staff and volunteers at their organization know which individuals are CSWs. Seven of the organizations require some type of open identification that distinguishes CSWs from other staff and volunteers, such as a vest, wristband, or special colored t-shirt. This is not surprising, given that open identification is technically required by the Dogwood Office. As one manager said, "Oh yeah ... Our CSWs are required to be identified as community service workers. That's one of the [Dogwood Office's] rules. They have to wear a [special] t-shirt, and they have to buy it. Whereas we give t-shirts or nametags to volunteers" (Emma). Some organizations that did not work with the Dogwood Office, though, also instituted this policy. For example, one recreation organization specified that the purpose of using special vests for CSWs was not to distinguish them from staff or other volunteers but to distinguish them from clients using the recreation areas. An additional five volunteer managers reported that everyone knows who the CSWs are because they are introduced as CSWs but are not required to wear any type of identification. One manager summarized this by saying: "Probably because I would introduce them, Hey this is Leanne. She's going to be helping us today. She's doing her community service work" (Amelia). Thus, 40 percent of the organizations in our study openly identify CSWs to staff, volunteers, and clients.

The remaining organizations limited identification in some way. In eight organizations, only other staff members know who the CSWs are. The managers in these organizations felt that no one outside of the staff needed to know this information. "Staff do. Other volunteers do not. And that's a personal choice that I make. There's no organizational policy to say that we should or should not disclose who the court-ordered workers are ... I know that it's not good to stigmatize people who are coming to help your organization" (Asher). In fact, in some organizations, the only reason that CSWs were identified to staff was that staff members signed off on CSWs' time sheets. "In general, I try to inform them. Not because we treat them any differently but because of documentation purposes. Our volunteers sign themselves in and out. Our CSWs have to have a notation from a staff member" (Elijah). An additional four organizations limited awareness of CSW status to key staff members. Lucas described this process:

> I introduce them as a volunteer to everybody. Then I take the staff member who may need to know aside if there's something they need to know, like if they did something before that might be a hindrance to the program in some way. I don't try to differentiate because I don't want them to feel awkward in front of the staff.

Volunteer managers in these organizations did not want CSWs to be stigmatized or treated differently because of their involvement in the criminal legal system.

This also explains why the remaining six organizations did not broadcast the CSWs' status to staff, volunteers, or clients at all. As one manager said, "We treat them all the same" (Levi). The managers in these organizations did not see any compelling reason why CSWs needed to be identified as such and wanted to protect their privacy. However, a couple of these managers did admit that others in the organization might know who a CSW is based on the tasks the individual is performing or because the CSWs themselves reveal that information. One manager described it this way, "I think in rare cases, that might come up just because that volunteer who is court-ordered might say something about being court-ordered in the presence of other volunteers or staff. But, yeah, I try not to say anything about why anyone is volunteering" (Luna). This type of disclosure was more likely in the organizations that received many CSWs, especially at the same time. One manager at a thrift store described this phenomenon by saying, "Well, most people don't make it a secret. They don't seem to mind. We may have 2 or 3 in one day. ... They work together, and they'll discuss their problems and their cases with each other. I mean, they don't seem to be bothered by it." (Sophia). When several CSWs are working around each other, they feel less concerned about the potential stigma because others are having the same experiences.

4.4.4 Community Service Workers' Perspectives on Open Identification

CSWs had varied feelings about being identified as CSWs within the organization. Nine CSWs reported that they felt embarrassed to wear a visual indicator showing them to be CSWs. They felt that people labeled or stigmatized them because of that identification. One CSW, Luca, who wore a different t-shirt to show he was a CSW, reported that he felt that the open identification caused others in the organization to view him differently. He said: It definitely comes in with a negative connotation from the start. People are like, "Oh, you're here for community service." There are also some negativities that's like, "You're not really invested here . . . you're just here to put in hours and help out," but it's not like a personally demeaning thing. Another CSW, Hazel, who wore a lanyard indicating she was a CSW, felt stigmatized by the open identification:

> It was a little embarrassing at first. . . . I should say that I am a law-abiding citizen and that I pride myself on being that way, and the particular chain of events that led to my misdemeanor was really kind of based on a miscommunication. I'm not saying that I didn't deserve what I got . . . but it just doesn't represent the person that I am. I feel like . . . just be labeled, you know, as a community service worker because of a misdemeanor, but, as I said, I've gotten used to it.

These CSWs were uncomfortable with being identified in the organization as CSWs and were concerned about how others would react to them.

On the other hand, fifteen CSWs were indifferent to open identification. Gabriel, who wore a special CSW vest, reported, "It doesn't bother me. It wouldn't bother me if anyone knew I'm a recovering drug addict, and many people know because that is who I am." An additional two CSWs did not necessarily like the open identification, but they felt that it was something they deserved. For example, Violet, who wore a vest, put it this way, "It's fine with me. I mean that I've done wrong, and I'm trying to correct what I've done." The CSWs in our sample varied greatly in their feelings about being openly identified as CSWs. Some CSWs did not like it and felt that they were treated differently as a result. Others were more complacent and just viewed the open identification as part of their punishment.

4.4.5 Lessons Learned about Risk Management and Open Identification

Just as working with volunteers can pose risks to an organization (Graff, 2012; Jackson et al., 2019), working with CSWs can also bring risks. When working with volunteers, organizations are primarily concerned about harm to others, particularly clients, the loss or destruction of the organization's assets, and damage to the organization's reputation (Graff, 2012). Likewise, community organizations also worry about any liabilities that might stem from working with CSWs (Allen & Treger, 1990), particularly potential risks to the organization's staff or beneficiaries (McIvor, 1993a). One of the primary ways that the community organizations in our study minimized potential risks was to screen out CSWs who have been convicted of violent crimes, similar to community organizations in other countries (McIvor, 1993b). Organizations also develop policies about which types of tasks CSWs are permitted to do, which can help minimize risk.

Another way that some community agencies minimize risk is to identify CSWs openly to agency staff and volunteers. While this policy may help organizations to mitigate risk, there are also tradeoffs. Many of our managers were uncomfortable openly identifying CSWs, even when directed to do so by the probation office.

They felt that action was not congruent with the type of relationship they desired to have with their CSWs. The interviews with the CSWs also bear this out. While some CSWs were indifferent to open identification, about one-third of them felt embarrassed or stigmatized. This is not surprising given the known stigma associated with a criminal record (e.g., Hirschfield & Piquero, 2010). Stigma toward formerly incarcerated individuals affects their opportunities for employment and civic reintegration (Uggen et al., 2004, 2014). A similar stigma can also be projected onto CSWs, as evidenced by the fact that organizations perceive that their staff and clients might be uncomfortable around CSWs. Given this, open identification policies appear to be at odds with many of the intended goals of court-mandated community service.

Community organizations should be thoughtful and intentional when discussing an open identification policy. They should consider such factors as how many CSWs they have in the organization at a particular time, which offenses the organization allows, what tasks the CSWs do, how easy it is to supervise CSWs (depending on the physical layout, number of staff, etc.), and how much work it will be to enforce the open identification policy. For example, if an organization only accepts CSWs with traffic violations, then the risk of harm to clients is very low, and an open identification policy might do the organization and CSWs more harm than good. We argue that organizations that carefully think through these details will choose policies that are more supportive of their goals overall, both in terms of risk management and providing a productive, nurturing environment for CSWs.

In summary, preparing an organization to receive CSWs involves many important tasks, including understanding why the organization wants to work with CSWs, developing a relationship with the probation office, and developing policies to support working with CSWs. We find that community organizations often muddle through this phase, either through a lack of planning and vision or by developing overly strict policies that could be hindering their goals. We believe that community service programs would function better with more appropriate support and guidance from probation offices; many of the Dogwood Office's procedures could be beneficial if they were used more widely. Community organizations could also use guidance to help management have more thoughtful conversations about how to develop policies that would support their intentions and goals for working with CSWs, such as how to create meaningful work for CSWs while balancing the need for appropriate risk management.

5 Onboarding Community Service Workers

The second phase of working with CSWs is organizational onboarding, which starts with a screening process where the organization decides whether or not they accept a particular CSW. Once a CSW has passed through the screening process, they receive orientation and training to prepare them for their work.

5.1 Organizational and Community Service Worker Screening Procedures

Organizational screening is the process of determining whether the organization and a CSW are a good fit for each other. Part of the screening process for CSWs is determining which CSWs to admit into the organization based on their criminal offenses. However, community organizations sometimes employ other methods to help determine which CSWs might be the best fit for their organization. Community service workers also have some choice about where to do their community service work, and they have their own processes for figuring out which location might be the best fit for them. In this section, we overview both organizational and CSW processes for mutually determining when placement is a good fit.

5.1.1 Organizational Screening Procedures

In addition to screening by offense, six organizations engaged in further screening by asking CSWs to undergo a background check. These organizations typically also require background checks for their volunteers. The argument in favor of a background check was that the individual might have prior offenses. "My understanding based on the orientation at the county probation office is that they have a very limited capacity on background checks they are able to perform, so even if someone is coming to us with, for example, a DUI charge, there's nothing to say they don't have another charge in their background, so that's why." (Asher). On the other hand, a couple of organizations excluded CSWs from their required background check, presumably because they already knew that these individuals had a criminal record.

The financial and time cost of the background check further hindered CSWs from being matched to a community organization. One manager indicated that the cost of the background check ($35, paid by the CSW) precluded some CSWs from being able to do their community service hours at that organization (Aria). The time required to complete the background check was also an obstacle for some CSWs. One volunteer manger described it this way:

> So, sometimes we would get ones that were assigned to us that would contact us very last minute and like wanted to start that week with hours. But, because of the background check, it takes about a week to process once we do meet with them to fill out. So often, I would get calls from volunteers saying, "I need to get my hours done this week. When can I come?" ... We just wouldn't be able to take those individuals then. (Nova)

Background checks not only screened out individuals based on their past offenses, but conducting background checks also inadvertently screened out CSWs who could not pay or who lacked the time to undergo the process.

Some organizations also prescreened CSWs on the phone by explaining how the community service process worked at their organization, including the necessary paperwork, what hours the organization is open and able to receive CSWs, and the organization's policies. These volunteer managers indicated that this process was helpful in screening out CSWs who would not be available for daytime shifts or who felt that this organization was not compatible with their needs. It also helped screen out individuals who needed to complete an unrealistic number of community service hours in a very short period of time.

5.1.2 Community Service Workers' Perspectives on Selecting an Organization

When an individual is assigned to a community service sentence and receives information about the process, their first concern is finding a good organizational placement. While the Dogwood Office and Azalea Office both maintain lists of local organizations that work with CSWs, in practice, many CSWs pursued their own arrangements for service opportunities. Eight CSWs in our sample selected one of the listed organizations, but sixteen CSWs searched for an organization themselves and obtained permission from the probation office to work there. One reason for this was that the list of organizations provided by the probation offices contained outdated or limited options, which was frustrating to CSWs. Ethan related his struggles with finding an organization:

> When they (probation offices) handed me a list, it was outdated. When they give a list, most of the tasks involve a limited number of hours and tasks only like cleaning ... I had to call people (organizations), and they said, "Yeah, we're not accepting any more, or we're not doing that." You had to go and be able to advocate for yourself. However, there are a lot of probationers who cannot advocate for themselves. This is why they end up not doing the hours.

The probation officers seemed sensitive to the difficulty of finding an organizational placement because they often allowed CSWs to do their community service hours at organizations that had not been previously vetted. This scenario fits Henry's situation:

> The ones I ended up doing were not part of the list that my probation officer gave. When I first met with my probation officer, I mentioned there was some trouble in contacting the people who I was originally signed with, and I proposed another place ... and they said it was okay as long as I worked for a nonprofit, which it was.

As Ethan indicated, though, it is likely that some CSWs would quit trying to find a placement if it proved too difficult. Individuals with physical limitations or injuries (Aden and Owen), disabilities (Eleanor and Kai), and certain criminal offenses (Willow and Owen) faced additional barriers in finding a placement, and that sometimes required more hands-on assistance from the probation office.

CSWs selected organizations based on a variety of factors. First, prior experience with community service work and/or volunteering and recommendations from family members or friends influenced their selection of a community service site. Previous volunteering experiences helped them to choose organizations where they had a prior relationship and already understood the work environment and tasks involved (Luca, Camila, Chloe, and Ivy). Jackson, for example, performed work for a church because of his father's recommendation: "My dad goes to that church. He said that if I could just do volunteering work, that they had enough work around the church for me do." Second, by necessity, CSWs had to select an organization that offered service hours that fit with their work schedule. Scheduling flexibility was a critical factor, as CSWs have a limited time period in which they must complete their service hours, making the process particularly complicated for those who were employed. "I'm getting close to the end of my probation period, and I still have quite a few hours to complete. [My organization] is not open Friday through Sunday, and they also close early in the afternoon on the days that they are open. It just conflicts with my work schedule a lot. So, I'm trying to supplement the hours." (Hazel). The combination of scheduling challenges and the need to get a lot of community service hours done in a short period of time meant that fourteen CSWs in our sample performed community service at more than one organization.

The third factor influencing a CSW's choice of organization was accessibility. When asked why he chose a particular organization, Ezra answered, "It was close to where I lived at the time, and it seemed like it would be easier duty." Besides location, transportation was also an important part of accessibility. Ten CSWs indicated that they lacked transportation, which posed problems in completing their community service. For example, Maverick had his driver's license revoked, making it hard for him to get to the community service site.

> I need $605 to pay the fine for reinstatement to get my driver's license back, but with the hours I'm going to [my organization], I must first obtain a job. I have to walk 2.5 hours to get here and 2.5 hours to get back home. And I stay here for two hours. It is seven hours a day. I don't have any time to go out to look for a job. (Maverick)

Finally, Wyatt, Henry, and Ivy indicated that they chose an organization because the tasks they would be performing fit their skills or interests.

To summarize, most CSWs sought out an organization for community service that was not on the list they received from the probation office. Typically, when they would look for an organization on their own, it was an organization that they or someone in their network had a prior relationship with. Community service workers were frustrated with the limited number of organizations where they could do community service, outdated lists of organizations, and few weekend and evening opportunities for community service. Community service workers with certain offenses were further limited in their community service opportunities.

5.1.3 Lessons Learned about Screening and Matching

Our results show the importance of screening to ensure that CSWs are matched with the right community organizations. This fits with prior volunteering research showing that effective recruitment, screening, and matching of volunteers to an organization can significantly increase volunteer satisfaction and reduce retention problems (Boezeman & Ellemers, 2008; Cuskelly et al., 2006; Hager & Brudney, 2008, 2011). The volunteer management literature highlights several reasons why screening volunteers is important (Connors, 2011; Jackson et al., 2019). First, screening is part of risk management and helps protect the organization's clients, staff, and assets. Screening techniques, including background checks, are very common among organizations that work with vulnerable populations, such as children and the elderly. The second major purpose of screening is to find volunteers who are a good fit for the organization, its mission, and the work. Screening ensures that volunteers are capable of the work the organization needs to have done and that the organization meets the needs of the volunteers. When these conditions are met, volunteers are happier, and they stay with the organization longer (Boezeman & Ellemers, 2008; Cuskelly et al., 2006; Hager & Brudney, 2008, 2011), which reduces the burden of recruiting and training additional volunteers. Screening can also increase staff members' willingness to work with volunteers because it can increase the overall quality of the volunteer corps.

Screening CSWs can serve similar functions. Screening can help reduce risk, ensure a better fit between the CSW and the organization, and increase staff willingness to work with CSWs. As previously discussed, the primary screening in our study is the screening out of prospective CSWs based on the offenses they committed. There is far more that organizations can do, though, in the screening process. For example, several volunteer managers utilized a prescreening phone call to set expectations for CSWs and to ensure that a potential CSW's schedule would work with the organization's schedule. Managers learned through experience that prescreening was important for avoiding problems of fit (e.g., scheduling, attitude). They also weeded out CSWs who procrastinated getting in their service hours and had an unreasonable number of hours to complete in a very short period of time. Several managers learned through their own experiences that there is value in the practitioner literature's recommendations around screening (Connors, 2011; Jackson et al., 2019). That said, screening procedures can also be taken too far and create unnecessary barriers that disempower CSWs and create more burdens for staff (Gaskin, 2003). Therefore, we argue that screening should be approached thoughtfully and intentionally so that organizations adopt the least invasive screening procedures that help set their CSWs up for success.

Likewise, CSWs are also screening organizations. Whereas volunteers often choose their volunteering opportunities based on the organization's mission or the type of work they will do (Brodie et al., 2011; Mitchell & Clark, 2020), CSWs are much more pragmatic. They focus on finding community service opportunities that fit their schedule and are accessible and convenient. As previously mentioned, it is frustrating for CSWs to receive inaccurate lists of organizations from the probation offices, which forces them to broker their own community service opportunities. When CSWs felt that their opportunities were limited, they often became discouraged, frustrated, or disillusioned – and might stop trying to complete their service hours altogether.

Essentially, we found that the process of screening and matching CSWs to organizations is not efficient. Community service workers and community organizations have different expectations about the service experience, and it takes some time and managerial effort to align those expectations. This sometimes creates negative experiences for both the community organizations and CSWs. Probation offices could do more to ensure a smoother matching process for CSWs and community organizations, particularly helping CSWs to understand the expectations associated with community service, working with a broader range of organizations to provide more opportunities for CSWs, keeping organizational listings updated, and promoting better communication. Additionally, community organizations need to be clear about the goals of their CSW program and adopt those screening procedures that support their goals with minimal burdens to staff and CSWs.

5.2 Orientation and Training

We found that CSWs received very little orientation and training as part of the onboarding process. Some organizations have the CSWs fill out an application or registration form (Olivia, Mia, Iris, Harper, Nova, Aria). A couple of organizations asked CSWs to sign a confidentiality agreement (Nova) or sign that they received and read the volunteer handbook (Aria). The most typical onboarding procedure was a short in-person orientation in which the manager would verbally share the organization's policies and procedures. Given that most of the CSWs perform simple manual labor, like cleaning, there was relatively little training involved. Training was typically handled on the job, at the time in which CSWs were asked to perform a task. One organization required that CSWs attend a training on client protection (Aria). Generally speaking, CSWs would be put straight to work soon after entering the organization.

5.2.1 Community Service Workers' Perspectives on Orientation and Training

Though several managers reported conducting orientations with CSWs, few CSWs remembered any type of orientation to their community service work. In our sample, only four CSWs indicated that they attended an orientation at the organization. Henry provided a brief overview of his orientation: "The orientation lasted an hour. They talked about an overview of the organization and then an overview of the different ways to spend your volunteer hours, and then they gave us a tour of the place and then answered any questions we had. After that, I guess, we were able to start doing volunteer hours there." The orientations focused mostly on informing CSWs about the organization, including information about how to record and report their community service hours. Aden's description of his orientation highlights this focus: "Basically, the rules and regulations, rights, and basic information about the expectations they have of the community service worker, including punctuality, scheduling, and just general information about community service hours and how they'd be handled, where to sign in, and the process to send it to your probation officer." These orientations were typically handled one-on-one between the manager and the CSW.

Despite the use of orientations, few CSWs remembered receiving any detailed information about the organization's mission and how their work would contribute to that mission. Only three CSWs felt that the orientation helped them to understand the community organization and its mission. Ethan recounted the thoroughness of his orientation:

> They had a booklet. It actually didn't happen on the first day. The first day I got there, I was just walking in, didn't know what I was walking into ... I would say about the third or fourth day when I was there, the manager asked me a bunch of questions and gave me an outline of what [the organization] was. It was a booklet of ... like what you'd give to an employee, actually. It was more of an employee orientation. I could understand who they were and where they fit at.

This experience of receiving information about the organization was not common among our sample of CSWs, however. The lack of a thorough orientation meant that CSWs did not fully understand or appreciate the work these organizations do in the community. For example, even after one CSW fulfilled forty hours of service in one organization, he still felt confused about what the organization actually does. He reported, "I didn't really have any idea what the organization (a veteran's organization) was about. I am a veteran, so I guess they expect me to know about it, but it's not. . . . You figure it out when you are there" (Ezra). This is potentially a missed opportunity. The organizations either seemed to assume that CSWs would know how their labor was benefiting the community, or it didn't really matter to them that CSWs understood their organization and its mission.

Additionally, few CSWs reported receiving any training; they mostly went straight to work. As Henry stated, "There was no [training]. I just started doing it." When asked if she received any training before doing her community service, Hazel replied, "I didn't get any actually. I showed up on my first day, and I was put straight to work. I was given a broom and told to sweep." It is possible that the lack of formal training was due to the simplicity of CSWs' tasks, such as cleaning. Nonetheless, failure to properly onboard CSWs is problematic.

5.2.2 Lessons Learned about Orientation and Training

The volunteer management literature indicates that providing volunteers with orientation and training will help ensure a smooth transition, increase the volunteers' comfort and confidence, and ensure that volunteers understand the organization's rules, policies, and procedures (Connors, 2011; Jackson et al., 2019). Effective orientation and training increases volunteers' satisfaction and commitment to the organization (Hager & Brudney, 2011). Unfortunately, structured onboarding procedures for volunteers have not been widely adopted in the nonprofit sector (Hager, 2004; Hager & Brudney, 2008). We found the same to be true regarding CSW onboarding; community organizations did not put much time and thought into procedures that would prepare CSWs for their work.

This underinvestment in orientation and training represents a missed opportunity. Prior research shows the importance of good onboarding for volunteer satisfaction and retention (Cuskelly et al., 2006; Hager & Brudney, 2004; Prince & Piatak, 2022). Cable et al. (2013) believe that onboarding can be an opportunity to invite newcomers to express their best selves in the workplace and to identify the strengths they bring to their work. Onboarding also helps to align volunteers' expectations with the organization's expectations (Hager & Renfro,

2020). It is likely that strong orientation and training would not only ensure that CSWs transition more smoothly into the organization, but it could increase their satisfaction with their role. Additionally, orientation can provide a critical bridge to help CSWs see and understand how the work they are doing for the organization is benefitting their community. Without an understanding of the organization's mission, CSWs might just feel like they are cleaning bathrooms rather than contributing to a greater cause. Onboarding is a way to help them see why the work they do is valuable because they will understand how the organization they are helping is benefiting and serving other people. Good onboarding might also help CSWs to get excited about serving their community and make them want to continue to contribute positively to their community in the future.

In a nutshell, the community organizations in our sample invested very little in good onboarding practices. Screening practices varied widely by organization and did not seem to be well-designed to support the organizations' goals for their CSW program. The community organizations desired more help from probation offices to prescreen CSWs so that they could avoid getting CSWs who would be unreliable or difficult workers. While CSWs might not need much training for the type of work they are currently doing, a strong orientation could help CSWs to better understand these mission-based organizations and could help them to feel more positively toward the work they are doing.

6 Creating a Supportive Environment for Community Service Workers

The final phase of our framework is creating a supportive environment for CSWs. This encompasses the CSW's relationship with their manager and with the rest of the staff. We include recognition and appreciation as another important component of a supportive work environment.

6.1 Relationships between the Manager and Community Service Workers

For many CSWs, their most important relationship at the organization is with the person who brings them into the organization and supervises their work. This relationship can make or break the experience for both CSWs and the manager. When situating CSWs in an organizational context, it is important to state that the primary difference between CSWs and volunteers is their motivation for providing unpaid labor to an organization. Volunteers are there, by definition, of their own volition. Community service workers are required to be there. The vast majority of CSWs in our sample said that completing their community service hours was a high priority. They were highly motivated because they knew that significant penalties, including jail time, could be levied if they did not complete their service hours. They wanted the burden of community service lifted so that they could move forward with their lives. As Carter stated, "Get it done, get off probation, and I can go back to normal life. As normal as can be." While CSWs do not have volunteers' intrinsic motivation to show up and help, many of them can still be productive, committed workers. However, the possibility also exists that some CSWs will try to shirk and avoid their work due to their lack of intrinsic motivation to do community service in this context. Because of this, we felt that it was important to understand how the managers perceived CSWs compared to the volunteers with whom they have worked.

6.1.1 Managers' Assessments of Community Service Workers Compared to Volunteers

There were a variety of opinions among managers regarding how CSWs compared to volunteers. Seven managers reported that the CSWs at their organizations were really no different than the organization's volunteers. As one manager stated, "Well, really, I can't tell any difference in them. Most of them come in, do their hours, and they're very polite. If you didn't know which one was which, you really wouldn't know" (Olivia). Another manager indicated, "All the court-ordered that I've had have been very pleasant. I don't see any attitude difference between them and my regular volunteers" (Isabella). A couple of the managers indicated that part of the reason for this was their attention to management details. One manager acknowledged the importance of proper orientation in getting this result, "My court-ordered folks are very reliable. I wouldn't give them 100%, but I'd give them a 90%. That's what my regular volunteers get. Stuff happens. As long as I do the groundwork when I meet with them and tell them the expectations, they 80/20 usually live up to it" (Elijah). Good screening and onboarding practices helped to increase CSW reliability.

However, nineteen managers reported that CSW quality relative to other volunteers was very mixed and highly dependent upon individual personalities. One manager described it this way, "Sometimes they're better, and sometimes they're worse. They're forced to be here; they don't choose to be here, so that can kind of be a 50/50 shot. ... They have some really good ones that try really hard and want to get their hours over with, and then there are others that drag it out" (Mateo). Several managers made similar comments – that some of their CSWs were great and either on par with or even better than their volunteers, but other CSWs were unreliable or difficult to work with. Managers' complaints about CSW behavior typically focused on a lack of enthusiasm for the work, not showing up when they are supposed to, or shirking behaviors. One manager described the difference between CSWs and volunteers this way:

> We will have some (CSWs) that come, and you have to say, 'Do that. Do this.' You know? When you go back there, if they have a chance, they'll be sitting there on their cell phone. But we have others who will actually look for things to do. They like to stay busy and do the job. Most of the time, a volunteer, if they're gonna take their time to volunteer, they're gonna come in and stay busy. You're not gonna have to tell them everything to do. (Olivia)

In Olivia's opinion, CSWs were more likely to waste time or shirk relative to volunteers. Several managers acknowledged that due to these issues, they have to supervise their CSWs more closely than their volunteers. "They'll stand around if you let them. They need more supervision than the others. There's definitely a difference there" (Evelyn). Typically, those CSWs who demonstrated issues regarding reliability, attitude, or work quality would either self-select out of the organization or be told not to come back. "The ones that aren't motivated usually don't last very long" (Eva). So, while unreliability and shirking were issues for these organizations, they typically would not put up with those issues for long.

While these types of issues were common, particularly for those organizations that use large numbers of CSWs, several of the managers believed that these challenges were due to differences across people and not just the uniqueness of court-ordered community service.

> I would say most of our court-ordered volunteers, 50% are pretty reliable that when they say they're going to be here on these hours, that's when they're going to be here. But we have had a good number of court-ordered volunteers who just don't show up to a shift, or they want hours, but then they just show up whenever, but I think that's reflective of people's personalities and not necessarily that they're court-ordered. (Luna)

Another manager, Emma, commented, "It's hard because we get so many CSWs and have so many unique experiences with them. It's hard to generalize." A few managers were also quick to point out that their volunteers are not flawless and that they too can be unreliable and unmotivated, so issues of reliability and quality are not isolated to CSWs.

> We need the help. I found that CSW, like any other population, runs the 80/20 rule. Eighty percent of them do great. Twenty percent of them not so much. But, typically, 80+% of the folks that come to work for us provide exceptional work. They do very well for us with a minimum amount of supervision, and that's what makes them worth doing the paperwork and bureaucracy to do that. . . .

> The 80/20 thing applies to my volunteers, too. Eighty percent of my volunteers
> are great, and twenty percent of my volunteers are troublesome. (Elijah)

Thus, some managers see volunteers and CSWs as comparable, with variation in both groups.

What is particularly interesting is that several managers commented that, in some way, their CSWs were better than their volunteers. In particular, these managers rated CSWs highly in terms of reliability. "I think our volunteers who come on a regular weekly basis, they are reliable to a point where they're gonna come. But, as far as making sure they're here and tending to a required time, the CSWs are better at that" (Lucas). One manager pointed out that CSWs are more reliable because of the consequence of unreliability.

> They're fairly reliable since they have to get the hours done by a certain date.
> They tend to sign up and show up. Volunteers tend to miss a lot of their
> scheduled shifts, but they're also not punished for doing so. If they sign up
> and don't show up then, oh well. But with community service after a couple
> of no-shows, we tend to realize and jump on them about that. (Mateo)

These managers also appreciated CSWs' willingness and compliance. "Yes, they're much more reliable. If they tell me they're gonna be here, they're here. I would underline that if I could. They are much more reliable. They're more dedicated to the work. They're more thorough with any task that I give. They're more eager to please" (Isabella). Another manager backed up Isabella's statement by saying, "They've been very much reliable, dependable, and usually perform tasks without having any issues or complaints about it. I've never had a court-ordered volunteer complain about anything they've done for me . . . I can't say that about general volunteers" (Levi). For these organizations, CSWs were even more valuable than volunteers because of their compliance, reliability, and willingness. It is important to note, though, that this value is in large part a result of the negative consequences that CSWs face if they fail to complete their community service. Thus, there is an element of coercion involved in the high performance that CSWs deliver to community agencies.

6.1.2 Managers' Orientation toward Management of Community Service Workers

Managers generally viewed CSWs' work quality as comparable to that of volunteers, with some CSWs being more difficult than volunteers and others being easier. It is not surprising, then, that we identified two main themes regarding how the managers viewed their management role – either a professional orientation with strict enforcement of the rules or a more nurturing, accommodating, relationship-based approach.

Some managers worked to run a tight, yet still reasonable, operation through a focus on rules and procedures. They saw themselves as enforcing the organization's and probation office's rules and ensuring that community service hours were being completed.

> Volunteers can essentially do whatever they want to do. We're just thankful to have them there. But, community service workers we have a lot of rules. They can't smoke. They can't be on their cell phone. That's actually a [Dogwood Office] rule; they were really strict about that one. They don't really take breaks. So, they're required to work 4 hours at a time. (Emma)

A couple of managers (Oliver and Emma) said that they have to be strict with the CSWs in order to ensure their compliance with the rules. This style of management was often emotionally detached from the CSWs. Charlotte perfectly encapsulated this professional – yet impersonal – approach to managing CSWs. "Generally speaking, with our volunteers, we've developed personal relationships with them because we see them so often and have a common goal. Community Service we generally don't build any kind of relationship with. They're here to do a job. We leave it at that." For these managers, a focus on enforcing rules was the way to successfully manage many CSWs so that they produced a net gain for the organization rather than being a drain on the organization's staff.

Other managers took a more relational approach to their CSWs. They were interested in the personal growth and future success of the CSWs and sought to encourage and help them. Volunteer managers at these agencies tended to view the CSWs as people who could be enlightened through sufficient support, education, and positive experiences like community service. Oliver's statement captures this management style perfectly:

> Because, I'm gonna say it like this okay … When they come in, this is how you carry yourself. I'm not a bully person. I talk to them nice. I say, "You know what? Make something out of your life. Be something." With everybody, I have something good to say. … Whenever I go to the foodbank or to pick up things, I carry one with me and I talk to them like a father talking to his son. That helps them a lot you know.

Unlike the more professional managers who treated CSWs as temporary labor, volunteer managers with a more parental orientation made a deeper emotional investment in the workers. They saw themselves as helping to rehabilitate CSWs and encouraging them to make better choices, just like a parent. As Amelia said, "Everyone treated them like they were their own children. Our thoughts were these kids made a wrong decision and wanted to put it behind them. Let's help them out." This more parental management style was more common for managers who said that working with CSWs fit their organization's mission.

These two orientations to management were not mutually exclusive. Managers would sometimes adapt to a more rigid or flexible style depending on the specific work environment, CSW, and situation. They would alter and vary their style as necessary to make their community service programs work effectively. Certainly, the choice of strategy would depend upon the CSWs themselves and how cooperative, responsive, and reliable they were.

6.1.3 Community Service Workers' Attitudes toward Managers

Community service workers generally reported positive feelings about their managers. Several of them described their manager as "great" (Hudson), "good" (Eliana), or "amazing" (Penelope). Some CSWs even reported that they developed a strong enough relationship with their manager that they would continue to help them if they were asked to do so:

> Yeah, I met, uh . . . the guy [the manager] at the [organization]; he's my buddy now, I guess. You know, I could say he's a friend. Actually, I would go back and help him if he needed me to help him . . . so if called me and said, "Hey I need help with something," I would do it for free. (Ezra)

When CSWs had a poor relationship with the manager, however, it negatively affected their overall work experience, as Jackson describes, "At first, I really liked [my volunteer manager]. . . . She was really nice, and I could talk to her, and she was really relaxed and everything. I don't know what changed, but at the very end, she kind of turned sour, so it was not a pleasant experience after that." Due to the manager's importance in supervising CSWs, they can have a disproportionate influence on CSWs' experiences within the organization – either positively or negatively.

6.1.4 Lessons Learned about Manager/Community Service Worker Relationships

Our findings make it clear that management matters. The relationship between the CSW and the manager is important and often contributes to what the CSWs report as either their most positive or most negative experiences. This is consistent with the volunteer management literature. Volunteers who feel that they receive adequate supervision and communication tend to give more hours and stay longer with the organization (Hidalgo & Moreno, 2009; Huynh et al., 2012; Kim et al., 2007; Studer, 2016). Once again, managers interested in working effectively with CSWs should be mindful of their supervisory techniques and ensure that they are providing adequate communication.

While we did not explicitly explore whether there was a relationship between assessments of CSW quality and the use of different managerial strategies, it is possible that the two are linked. On the basis of leader–member exchange theory and supporting evidence in the volunteer management literature (Mayr, 2017; Prince & Piatak, 2022; Schneider & George, 2011; Schreiner et al., 2018), we postulate that managers choose their managerial strategies according to their past and current experiences with CSWs and their assessment of CSW quality. The manager's own psychological needs, motivation, and previous working experiences (Rogelberg et al., 2010) can affect how the manager interacts and communicates with other staff and volunteers; this is likely true for CSWs, too. Managers who believe that most CSWs are lazy and difficult will adopt more rigid strategies and styles relative to managers who have more compassionate understanding views of CSWs and turn to more nurturing strategies. More research is needed to understand how managers' backgrounds and experiences with CSWs inform their management strategies and styles.

6.2 Relationships Between Staff and Community Service Workers

While CSWs' relationships with their manager are important, they also interact frequently with other staff as they do their community service. The quality of those interactions also shaped CSWs' experiences within the organization. Therefore, it is important to understand how staff and CSWs view and interact with each other.

6.2.1 Staff Attitudes toward Community Service Workers

We asked the managers to share their impressions of how the staff at their organizations feel about working with CSWs. Their responses were generally very positive. Eighteen volunteer managers indicated that their staff liked having CSWs (without adding qualifiers to that statement). In the words of one manager, "They enjoy it" (Noah). Another manager explained the staff's feelings by saying, "I think we all think it's a beneficial program. It's good for the community service worker; they're able to get their hours. We're able to get extra help" (Harper). The managers cited several reasons why their staff liked working with CSWs. One reason is that it saved staff from doing tasks that they did not want to do. As one manager, Gianna, said, "They love them . . . they can say, 'Hey, I don't want to sweep that floor over there, can you do it?'" In these organizations, staff generally appreciated having people helping with the work, and the managers encountered few problems between CSWs and staff. As one manager said, "Not once or ever [has there been a problem]. More than likely, it was because the ones [CSWs] we had were always so good, so polite, so willing to work, so willing to come and do whatever we needed with absolutely no problem" (Amelia).

Another six managers also responded that their staff liked working with CSWs, although they qualified their statement by saying that once in a while, they would have an issue. For example, the staff might get frustrated with CSWs when they slack on the job or during slower times when it is more difficult to find work for them. These volunteer managers also indicated that specific individuals or groups of employees might be more reluctant to work with CSWs, but the staff overall felt positive about it. The following response encapsulates this group well:

> I had one staff member out of this 100-member staff who was not pleasant about it. She wanted to use people for a heavy labor task once in a blue moon, but other than that, she wanted nothing to do with them. She resented having to document everything. Otherwise, everybody has been very pleasant because we are getting free labor. In most cases, we are getting more than free labor: free labor and some skills. (Elijah)

Still, despite small frustrations and specific employees being reluctant to work with CSWs, staff at these organizations were very willing to work with CSWs.

The remaining four volunteer managers described staff attitudes toward CSWs as a "mixed bag." While staff appreciated the help and valued CSWs with good attitudes and work ethics, they viewed dealing with CSWs as burdensome, especially when they have a bad attitude, break rules, or do not show up when scheduled. One volunteer manager described it this way:

> It depends. It's a mixed bag. We have had court-ordered volunteers who are amazing. They've got 40, 60 hours they need to do. They tell us, "This is what my schedule is. I have these 2 days off each week. I can come in." When they're in there, they're doing above and beyond. They're just getting the tasks done. They know they have an issue, and they're fixing it. Then, there are the ones that we never hear from. They're going to come in, and we wait for them, and they never come in. ... Then, we move on with the day. Basically, if you haven't shown up three times after you say you are gonna show up, we just tell you we don't need you anymore. It puts a lot on us. We will have jobs figured out for them to do, and then nobody is there to do it. It puts us behind. (Aurora)

Another volunteer manager described this as the "growing pains" of trying to help CSWs learn responsibility and discipline (Emma). In these organizations, the staff viewed CSWs more as "hit or miss" (Charlotte) in terms of their behavior and contribution to the organization. Interestingly, all of the managers that describe CSWs as a mixed bag represent organizations receiving large numbers of CSWs, which suggests that it is the volume of CSWs that is posing the challenge.

Several volunteer managers emphasized their critical role in making staff relationships with CSWs work. They emphasized that staff were cooperative as long as they knew that the volunteer manager would address any issues that arose. As one manager said, "My staff trusts that I will not allow court-ordered volunteers that have any type of record that would cause a problem for us" (Ella). Another manager stated, "They work well together. They know if they have a problem that I'll deal with it" (Oliver). Finally, one manager described this type of situation in more detail, saying:

> Yes, I think sometimes we will have some conflict. We have some people that come in that don't like to be told what to do. We've had to turn people away. We've had to have people removed. ... Sometimes, we have issues with somebody comes in high or drunk, and we will have to call the police and have them removed, so. There are issues that do cause our employees to be leery, but with that being said, as long as we deal with the problems as they come up, the program works really well. The employees are happy with the extra help, believe me. (Evelyn)

Thus, the volunteer managers acknowledge the critical role they play in ensuring good relationships between CSWs and staff.

6.2.2 Community Service Workers' Attitudes toward Staff

We asked CSWs how much they enjoy working with other people in the organization. Community service workers typically had far less interaction with other agency staff than they did with the volunteer manager, which made it difficult to develop relationships with the staff. The CSWs indicated that staff could be a bit mistrusting at first. Over time, CSWs could build trust with staff as they demonstrated their reliability and value to the organization. Ethan indicated how showing up consistently helped him to win over the staff:

> I would say it took about two months or a month of being there before they got over their natural cynicism that accompanies having to handle that many, um, demands from people doing community service. ... As soon as I was consistent, they got to know me personally. After I was consistent . . . the typical community service person is random, they just show up. They'll say they're gonna come back and they don't. . . . When I got consistent, they got nice.

At the same time, CSWs acknowledged that staff might not want to spend the time to get to know them since their time at the organization would be short. As Luca described, "You're not there every day, and they know that there's no longevity with it. Thus, the investment in internal relationships is less than what a normal staff would have. That makes sense to me" (Luca). Due to the temporary nature of community service and the number of CSWs coming through the organization, staff were reluctant to get to know them personally.

Despite this, several CSWs felt positively inclined toward the staff and felt that they were pleasant to work with. As Hunson said, "They don't make me feel like I'm doing community service at all ... I just feel like I'm there helping." Another CSW, Hazel, worked in one human service nonprofit for more than a hundred hours and reported positive interactions with the staff: "They're very welcoming and very attentive to the CSWs. I never feel like I'm left in the dark or I don't know what I'm supposed to be doing. There's always someone there I can go to and ask questions." Some CSWs viewed community service as a positive experience because of their positive interactions with staff.

Yet some CSWs did not feel that they were treated well at their organizations, sometimes being marginalized by the staff. Henry recounted his experience, "Uh, there's been one day of lifting stuff or moving heavy stuff for one of the people, and they wouldn't look at me or even kind of address me. They would just like ... that was it, used to go there ... kind of like treating me like a servant, I guess." Henry's quote makes it sound like the staff was not friendly toward or inclusive of the CSWs. Some CSWs had some troubling conversations or interactions with the organization's staff or clients, such as being pressured about their political views (Sebastian) or religious views (Mason).

6.2.3 Lessons Learned about Staff/Community Service Worker Relationships

Volunteer and staff relationships are crucial for the success of any volunteer program, and our results show the same is true for organizations working with CSWs. Our findings indicate that what is true for volunteers is also true for CSWs – positive social integration into the organization is key for positive outcomes (Cuskelly et al., 2006; Einolf, 2018; Galindo-Kuhn & Guzley, 2001). Positive relationships not only make the CSW happier and more likely to be pleasant and reliable, but it also supports staff willingness to work with CSWs. Some minor conflict between staff and CSWs is to be expected – just as it is in any arena of human interaction. The volunteer management literature provides ample evidence of tensions between volunteers and staff due to divergent expectations, communication challenges, job ambiguity, and personality conflicts (MacDuff, 2012; Pearce, 1993; Rimes et al., 2017; Wandersman & Alderman, 1993). Unhealthy relationships between staff and volunteers are associated with lower satisfaction levels and increased turnover among staff and volunteers (Hobson, 2007; Kulik, 2006; Rogelberg et al., 2010). The same is also true for CSWs. Tension between staff and CSWs will lead CSWs to quit or become more difficult to work with and will cause staff to resist working with CSWs.

Organizations should not assume that good relationships between staff and CSWs will happen on their own. Good managerial support and thoughtful policies and procedures help to set CSWs and staff up for success. Implementing best practices for organizations that rely on volunteers could also benefit organizations working with CSWs, such as training staff to work with CSWs, facilitating open communication, and quickly addressing any conflict between staff and CSWs (Nesbit, 2024). Our results show the importance of having a watchful manager address concerns regarding a problematic CSW (or staff member) to maintain a welcoming culture for CSWs. Robust onboarding practices also support good relationships because it helps to clarify expectations for CSWs. Staff have a profound impact on CSWs' perceptions of their community service experience, so it is important that community organizations intentionally support these relationships.

6.3 Recognition and Appreciation

The final part of creating a supportive environment for CSWs is providing recognition and appreciation to the CSWs, just as organizations would do with volunteers. A majority of the CSWs reported that they had been thanked in some way by someone at the organization. The most typical form of appreciation was a quick verbal "thank you" at the end of a shift. As Jackson said, "It wasn't like a big, they never did anything, but they would say like alright thanks, you can go home." A couple CSWs talked about more significant ways that they received recognition from their host organization. Ethan reported that the organization had a big party. Another CSW reported that the staff made her feel important and valued through their expressions of gratitude:

> Yeah, they'll say, um, things like, oh, you know, wow, I don't know how we could have gotten through today because it was so busy without your help, like thank you so much, um, I am always so happy when you walk through the door because I know it's gonna be a good day. Things like that, and that . . . that really means a lot to me. (Hazel)

Yet despite these positive experiences, some CSWs reported that they were never thanked for the work they did for the organization. Luca said, "The physical words [thank you] have not been spoken."

While most CSWs were thanked in some way for their contributions, few indicated that they received any type of positive feedback about their work. Most CSWs indicated that they were never told that they were doing a good job or provided with other helpful reports on their work quality. For some CSWs, receiving positive feedback was so rare that those instances when they did receive such feedback stood out as memorable experiences. Willow described her positive experience doing her service hours:

> "There were a couple of times with the customers and went to the manager and told I was an excellent help in finding what they needed." Simple positive feedback or showing appreciation helped CSWs feel valued, recognized, and satisfied despite doing community service as a punishment. Positive feedback helped the CSWs feel that they were doing something meaningful that they could take pride in.

Recognition is another potential missed opportunity for community organizations. The volunteer management literature has long touted the need for volunteer appreciation and recognition as a means of keeping volunteers happy and satisfied (Connors, 2011; Jackson et al., 2019). Volunteers who receive some type of thank you or recognition for their work are more satisfied and more likely to continue volunteering (Kulik, 2006; Wisner et al., 2005). Organizations that regularly recognize volunteers' contributions experience fewer issues while recruiting and retaining volunteers (Hager & Brudney, 2004, 2011). Despite this, few CSWs in our sample reported that they were regularly recognized for their contributions and even fewer reported receiving positive feedback. More recognition and appreciation for their efforts could make CSWs happier and help them feel that they are doing something to benefit their community. It is even possible that better recognition efforts could reduce some of CSWs' less helpful behaviors and attitudes by making them feel that what they do is valued by the organization, its staff, and its beneficiaries.

The last phase of working with CSWs comprises creating a supportive environment, particularly focusing on CSWs' relationships with their managers and with other staff. Most of the organizations in our study work with CSWs because they need people who can do basic labor for them, but that rationale combined with stigma associated with involvement in the criminal legal system can easily lead organizations and their staff to take CSWs for granted and to treat them more like servants than like community members who are giving their time to a cause. The more that organizations treat their CSWs with respect – by facilitating positive relationships within the organization and recognizing and appreciating their contributions – the more successful their work with CSWs will be.

7 Increasing the Value of Community Service Work

This study describes how community organizations and CSWs experience each other through community service. While court-ordered community service is often painted as a win-win solution that simultaneously provides labor to community organizations and reduces incarceration, we find that this view is simplistic. Instead, court-ordered community service poses a managerial conundrum: Do community organizations merely use CSWs' labor, or do they invest in developing a more mutually beneficial relationship?

7.1 Volunteer Management Capacity is Key for Effective Community Service

To understand how community agencies manage CSWs, we have examined the experiences of organization staff and CSWs through the lens of the volunteer management literature. Though not all volunteer-focused organizations adhere to best practices in managing volunteers (Hager, 2004; Hager & Brudney, 2008), the well-established literature on volunteer management provides benchmarks against which nonprofit organizations can be evaluated. Community service workers, however, are not volunteers. While they may have some choice regarding the organizations in which they fulfill their required hours, CSWs are working *involuntarily*. Their status as conscripted laborers greatly complicates the relationship between CSWs and the organization in which they are fulfilling their hours. In framing the experiences of CSWs and the agencies who use their labor within the volunteer management literature, we are implicitly asking whether findings about how to manage volunteers also apply to management of a nonvolunteer workforce, as well as whether it is feasible to manage a volunteer and nonvolunteer workforce simultaneously.

Our findings suggest that adherence to volunteer management best practices can lead to better overall experiences for CSWs and community agencies, but that there are additional factors to consider when working with CSWs. This begins with a clear understanding of why the organization is taking on CSWs, just as an organization must establish a rationale for utilizing a volunteer workforce. The most common rationale was a simple need for the labor that CSWs supplied, while a few agencies saw working with CSWs as consistent with their mission. These rationales shaped the way in which managers treated CSWs, for better or for worse. We assert that those organizations whose rationale includes helping and giving back to CSWs – along with receiving some beneficial labor – will have more successful CSW programs because this rationale will lead them to adopt practices that support CSW involvement.

Designing the work for CSWs is another crucial step. Many of the organizations in our sample had a high need for basic labor, especially thrift stores and animal shelters. However, we suggest that providing CSWs with opportunities for meaningful work, such as helping clients, will lead to better outcomes than will assigning them manual labor alone. This would provide CSWs with a more rewarding experience and lead to more reliability and better work quality for community organizations. The organizations in our study put very little thought and effort into developing meaningful work for CSWs (as they would for volunteers), yet they lamented that CSWs would not show up for their shifts or would shirk their work. More thoughtful work design could potentially alleviate some of those problems. The volunteer management literature also supports reflection as an indicator of intention to continue volunteering because it allows volunteers to make sense of their experiences as they do their volunteer work (Wisner et al., 2005). Providing CSWs with opportunities to reflect on their experiences might also help them to see more meaning and purpose in their community service work.

Just as with volunteers, there is a mutual screening process for CSWs and community agencies. We found that this process was inefficient, partly due to probation offices' inaccurate records. Beyond that, there were often mismatches between a probationer's offense and the offenses an organization would accept. Mismatches between the probationer's schedule and the organization's operating hours were also common. In communities with few opportunities for community service work, these mismatches could lead CSWs to be noncompliant with their community service requirements – something that the court systems need to be aware of before assigning community service. Screening is necessary, however, because it is part of the process of aligning the needs and expectations of community organizations and their CSWs. Yet, organizations must ensure that screening does not pose unnecessary barriers for CSWs or create excessive burden for staff.

Though well-developed orientations and trainings have been found to increase volunteer success (Cuskelly et al., 2006; Hager & Brudney, 2011), the agencies in our sample did not invest sufficiently in orientation and training for CSWs. This is a missed opportunity as the lack of the onboarding makes it difficult for the CSWs to feel connected to the organization or understand how their work is benefitting the community. Community organizations that view working with CSWs as an opportunity to recruit future volunteers and develop evangelists for their cause might be able to spark a new interest or passion within their CSWs – and that starts by helping them to understand the organization and its mission.

Community agencies must also create a supportive environment in order to maintain an effective volunteer workforce (Nesbit, 2024), and our research suggests that the same is true for CSWs. In recounting their best and worst agency experience, CSWs frequently referenced their relationship with the volunteer manager or other staff. Adoption of the volunteer management best practices, such as strong onboarding, leads to a more supportive environment.

We believe that if community organizations put the same amount of effort into recognizing and appreciating their CSWs as they do with their volunteers, they would experience better outcomes. Just because CSWs are required to do community service, they should not be treated less well than volunteers.

7.2 Challenges of Managing a Conscripted Workforce

There are many ways in which findings about how to manage a voluntary workforce also apply to management of CSWs, despite the nonvoluntary nature of CSWs' labor. At the same time, we also find that managing a voluntary and nonvoluntary workforce simultaneously is challenging for some managers, forcing them to utilize different strategies for these groups, while other managers report little difference in the ways they deal with volunteers and CSWs. We suspect, though, that some of this difficulty may be because the organizations in our study invested very little in a good volunteer management infrastructure in their organizations. As a result, it was difficult for them to build on this infrastructure to incorporate CSWs into their agencies. This problem is not unique to these organizations. Many volunteer-using organizations underinvest in their volunteer manager and only adopt a handful of the volunteer management best practices (Hager, 2004; Hager & Brudney, 2004, 2008). Rehnborg et al. (2009) describe a "cycle of poorly managed volunteer engagement" where organizations bring in volunteers but invest very little in supervising them. When volunteers fail to achieve the desired results, the organization blames them instead of its own lack of volunteer management ability.

We find that community organizations tend to underinvest in their CSWs, just as they do in their volunteers. This is despite the fact that the organizations in our study relied heavily on the labor that CSWs provide and recognized that CSWs had unique needs and constraints. Organizations that invest in the practices we described, such as good onboarding procedures and creating a welcoming environment, will likely experience fewer challenges working with CSWs than organizations that fail to make these investments. Likewise, we expect that CSWs will have better experiences when such practices are followed. It is likely that these practices will also benefit organizations that work with other "conscripted" volunteers. For example, many public housing agencies require housing recipients to do community service as a condition of receiving housing. Schools also often require students to "volunteer." These groups will also require a good volunteer management infrastructure to help them be successful.

Community organizations should also realize, however, that probation offices may not provide them with adequate policy guidance on which to build their CSW management infrastructure. We found that this was particularly true of private probation offices, which is troubling since private probation is on the rise (Phelps, 2020). Even state-run offices, though, may either fail to provide adequate guidance or provide guidance that is counter to the community organization's goals, such as when the probation offices require identification of the CSWs. Part of this neglect might be due to insufficient state funding that would allow probation offices to develop an infrastructure that sufficiently supports community service. When this occurs, it is incumbent on the community organizations to develop policies and procedures for working with CSWs that allow them to advance their mission while also providing CSWs with a fulfilling work experience, which is the same type of mutually beneficial relationship that community organizations seek to establish with their volunteers.

We assert that good volunteer management capacity, adoption of key best practices, and effective supervision can help promote a mutually beneficial relationship between community organizations and CSWs. A functional relationship with a well-prepared probation office also contributes to effective community service work. When these components are in place, court-ordered community service should function more smoothly and cause less stress for all the parties involved. If this groundwork is not in place, then it is unlikely that court-ordered community service is benefitting either the community or the CSWs.

7.3 Limitations and Directions for Future Research

One limitation of our research is that we interviewed volunteer managers and CSWs associated with only two probation offices. The primary objective of selecting two distinct jurisdictions – Dogwood, with its urban characteristics, and Azalea, reflecting a more rural setting – was to facilitate a comparative analysis. We found that these different jurisdictional contexts affected the experiences of community organizations and CSWs. However, these choices may not include the complete spectrum of variability across probation offices and jurisdictions, and we suspect there is wide variation nationally in the ways that community service programs are implemented by probation offices. Based on our results, we suspect that the Dogwood Office is atypically proactive and professional in their approach. This study acknowledges the limitations inherent in its scope, primarily due to constraints in data accessibility and the broader challenges of generalizing findings from two specific jurisdictions. Consequently, this research should be viewed as a preliminary exploration, offering insights that are valuable yet not exhaustive.

Additional organizational factors, including funding level, policy orientation, and historical context within the community, may uniquely shape the probation or court-ordered service experience, opening up more opportunities for future investigation. Ideally, further studies would extend to a broader range of jurisdictions, thereby facilitating a more comprehensive understanding of the landscape of community service programs. This study serves as a foundational step, setting the stage for more extensive research that could further elucidate the dynamics present across a wider spectrum of jurisdictions.

We also limited our sample to organizations currently working with CSWs. This means that organizations that have worked with CSWs in the past – and perhaps stopped doing so due to the challenges we discussed – are not represented in our sample. While our sample represents a variety of community organizations that differ in both size and mission, our data do not allow us to speak to the differences between those community organizations that work with CSWs and those that do not. Future research could help us to understand what factors cause an organization to start – and stop – working with CSWs and how and why that changes over time for a particular organization.

Future research should also examine the effectiveness of community service as a condition of probation. A full examination of this topic requires following CSWs through the course of their probation and a large and diverse enough sample to account for a variety of agency characteristics and experiences. At the very least, future research should consider whether agency representatives and CSWs, themselves, perceive that court-ordered community service is a worthwhile sentence. This type of investigation must acknowledge the net-widening effects of court-ordered community service, given the negative consequences of probation, more generally.

We found that community organizations are hungry for guidance and direction when working with CSWs. Community organizations need more practical support for working with CSWs. While the volunteer management literature provides a great foundation of support, we need more research to understand the nuances of working with CSWs and to develop a set of best practices for working with this unique population. Researchers and practitioners can do more to provide and promote evidence-based practices for community service and how to manage and support CSWs most effectively.

7.4 Conclusion

Throughout this Element, we have highlighted an important managerial conundrum for organizations working with CSWs – whether to merely "use" the labor of CSWs or whether to invest in them, as they should with volunteers. While CSWs may appear on the surface to be "free" labor, our study shows that in order to achieve a mutually beneficial relationship with CSWs, organizations must develop an organizational infrastructure that supports CSWs' work, just as with volunteers. Organizations also need to recognize the complications of using conscripted labor. Community service workers are not free, in any sense of the word. Yet, despite that, they can provide beneficial work to community organizations, and community organizations can provide them with a meaningful experience in return. We encourage community organizations to revisit their work with CSWs and strive to create more successful and productive relationships through application of best practices from the volunteer management literature.

References

Alfes, K., Shantz, A., & Bailey, C. (2016). Enhancing volunteer engagement to achieve desirable outcomes: What can non-profit employers do? *Voluntas: International Journal of Voluntary and Nonprofit Organizations, 27*(2), 595–617. https://doi.org/10.1007/s11266-015-9601-3.

Allen, G. F., & Treger, H. (1990). Community service orders in federal probation: Perceptions of probationers and host agencies. *Federal Probation, 54*(3), 8.

Anonymized Probation Office. (2018). *Supervising Community Service Workers Packet.*

Bauer, E. L., Crosse, S., McPherson, K., et al. (2014). *Evaluation of the New York City Justice Corps: Final Outcome Report.* Westat, Metis Associates.

Bazemore, G. (1991). New concepts and alternative practice in community supervision of juvenile offenders: Rediscovering work experience and competency development. *Journal of Crime and Justice, 14*(1), 27–52.

Bazemore, G., & Karp, D. (2004). A civic justice corps: Community service as a means of reintegration. *Justice Policy Journal, 1*(3), 1–35.

Bittschi, B., Pennerstorfer, A., & Schneider, U. (2019). The effect of volunteers on paid workers' excess turnover in nonprofit and public organizations. *Review of Public Personnel Administration, 39*(2), 256–275.

Boezeman, E. J., & Ellemers, N. (2008). Volunteer recruitment: The role of organizational support and anticipated respect in non-volunteers' attraction to charitable volunteer organizations. *Journal of Applied Psychology, 93,* 1013–1026. https://doi.org/10.1037/0021-9010.93.5.1013.

Bonczar, T. P. (1997). Characteristics of adults on probation, 1995. *Traffic, 4*(9), 10–12.

Boone, M. (2010). Only for minor offences: Community service in the Netherlands. *European Journal of Probation, 2*(1), 22–40.

Bouffard, J. A., & Muftic, L. R. (2006). Program completion and recidivism outcomes among adult offenders ordered to complete a community service sentence. *Journal of Offender Rehabilitation, 43*(2), 1–33. https://doi.org/10.1300/J076v43n02_01.

Brodie, E., Hughes, T., Jochum, V., et al. (2011). *Pathways through Participation.* London: NCVO, Involve, IVR.

Brown, B. (1977). Community service as a condition of probation. *Federal Probation, 41,* 7.

Brudney, J. L. (2010). Designing and managing volunteer programs. In D. O. Renz (Ed.), *The Jossey-Bass Handbook of Nonprofit Leadership and Management* (3rd ed., pp. 753–793). John Wiley & Sons.

Brudney, J. L. (2016). Designing and managing volunteer programs. In D. O. Renz & R. D. Herman (Eds.), *The Jossey-Bass Handbook of Nonprofit Leadership and Management* (4th ed., pp. 688–733). Jossey-Bass.

Brudney, J. L., & Meijs, L. C. (2014). Models of volunteer management: Professional volunteer program management in social work. *Human Service Organizations: Management, Leadership & Governance, 38*(3), 297–309.

Cable, D. M., Gino, F., & Staats, B. R. (2013). Reinventing employee onboarding. *MIT Sloan Management Review, 54*(3), 23.

Carter, R. M., Cocks, J., & Glaser, D. (1987). Community service: A review of the basic issues. *Federal Probation, 51,* 4.

Cohen, S. (2008). *The Responsible Contract Manager: Protecting the Public Interest in an Outsourced World.* Georgetown University Press.

Connors, T. D. (2011). *The Volunteer Management Handbook: Leadership Strategies for Success* (2nd ed.). Wiley.

Cuskelly, G., Taylor, T., Hoye, R., & Darcy, S. (2006). Volunteer management practices and volunteer retention: A human resource management approach. *Sport Management Review, 9*(2), 141–163.

DiMaggio, P., & Powell, W. W. (2010). The iron cage revisited: Institutional isomorphism and collective rationality in organizational fields (translated by G. Yudin). *Journal of Economic Sociology, 11*(1), 34–56. https://doi.org/10.17323/1726-3247-2010-1-34-56.

Doherty, F. (2016). Obey all laws and be good: Probation and the meaning of recidivism. *Georgetown Law Journal, 104*(2), 291–354.

Dünkel, F., & Lappi-Seppälä, T. (2014). Community service in Europe: Encyclopedia of criminology and criminal justice. In G. Bruinsma & D. Weisburd (Eds.), *Encyclopedia of Criminology and Criminal Justice* (pp. 426–442). Springer. https://doi.org/10.1007/978-1-4614-5690-2_567.

Dwyer, P. C., Bono, J. E., Snyder, M., Nov, O., & Berson, Y. (2013). Sources of volunteer motivation: Transformational leadership and personal motives influence volunteer outcomes. *Nonprofit Management and Leadership, 24*(2), 181–205.

Einolf, C. (2018). Evidence-based volunteer management: A review of the literature. *Voluntary Sector Review, 9,* 153–176. https://doi.org/10.1332/204080518X15299334470348.

Eisner, D., Grimm Jr., R. T., Maynard, S., & Washburn, S. (2009). The new volunteer workforce. *Stanford Social Innovation Review, 7*(1), 32–37.

Fallon, B. J., & Rice, S. M. (2015). Investment in staff development within an emergency services organisation: Comparing future intention of volunteers and paid employees. *The International Journal of Human Resource Management, 26*(4), 485–500.

Farmer, S. M., & Fedor, D. B. (2001). Changing the focus on volunteering: An investigation of volunteers' multiple contributions to a charitable organization. *Journal of Management, 27*(2), 191–211. https://doi.org/10.1177/0149206 30102700204.

Feeley, M. M., Berk, R., & Campbell, A. (1992). Between two extremes: An examination of the efficiency and effectiveness of community service orders and their implications for the US sentencing guidelines. *Southern California Law Review, 66*, 155.

Finkelstein, M. A. (2008). Volunteer satisfaction and volunteer action: A functional approach. *Social Behavior & Personality: An International Journal, 36*(1), 9–17.

Florida Department of Corrections. (2018). *2017–18 Annual Report*. Florida Department of Corrections. www.dc.state.fl.us/pub/index.html.

Frenzel, J. (2021). Recruitment, screening, and management: Volunteer staffing and development. In K. Seel & J. R. Bennett (Eds.), *Volunteer Administration: Professional Practice* (4th ed., pp. 121–144). LexisNexis Canada.

Galindo-Kuhn, R., & Guzley, R. M. (2001). The volunteer satisfaction index: Construct definition, measurement, development, and validation. *Journal of Social Service Research, 28*(1), 45–68.

Gaskin, K. (2003). *A Choice Blend: What Volunteers Want from Organisation and Management*. Institute for Volunteering Research.

Gazley, B., & Brudney, J. L. (2005). Volunteer involvement in local government after September 11: The continuing question of capacity. *Public Administration Review, 65*(2), 131–142. https://doi.org/10.1111/j.1540-6210.2005.00439.x.

Gelsthorpe, L., & Rex, S. (2004). Community service as reintegration: Exploring the potential. In G. Mair (Ed.), *What Matters in Probation* (pp. 229–254). Routledge.

Georgia Department of Community Supervision. (2017). *2017 Annual Report*. Georgia Department of Community Supervision. https://view.joomag.com/dcs-annual-report-2017/0227506001515682749?short.

Giguere, R., & Dundes, L. (2002). Help wanted: A survey of employer concerns about hiring ex-convicts. *Criminal Justice Policy Review, 13*(4), 396–408.

Graff, L. L. (2005). *Best of All: The Quick Reference Guide to Effective Volunteer Involvement*. Linda Graff and Associates.

Graff, L. L. (2012). Risk management in volunteer involvement. In T. D. Connors (Ed.), *The Volunteer Management Handbook* (2nd ed., pp. 323–360). John Wiley & Sons.

Grube, J. A., & Piliavin, J. A. (2000). Role identity, organizational experiences and volunteer performance. *Personality and Social Psychology Bulletin*, *26*(9), 1108–1119. https://doi.org/10.1177/01461672002611007.

Hager, M. A. (2004). *Volunteer Management Capacity in America's Charities and Congregations: A Briefing Report*. Urban Institute.

Hager, M. A., & Brudney, J. L. (2004). *Volunteer Management Practices and Retention of Volunteers*. The Urban Institute. www.urban.org/sites/default/files/publication/58001/411005-Volunteer-Management-Practices-and-Retention-of-Volunteers.PDF.

Hager, M. A., & Brudney, J. L. (2008). Management capacity and retention of volunteers. *Challenges in Volunteer Management*, *1*, 9–27.

Hager, M. A., & Brudney, J. L. (2011). Problems recruiting volunteers: Nature versus nurture. *Nonprofit Management and Leadership*, *22*(2), 137–157. https://doi.org/10.1002/nml.20046.

Hager, M. A., & Renfro, K. T. (2020). Volunteer management and the psychological contract. In H. Anheier and S. Toepler (Eds.), *The Routledge Companion to Nonprofit Management* (pp. 278–290). Routledge. www.taylorfrancis.com/chapters/edit/10.4324/9781315181011-22/volunteer-management-psychological-contract-mark-hager-kathy-renfro.

Harland, A. T. (1980). Court-ordered community service in criminal law: The continuing tyranny of benevolence. *Buffalo Law Review*, *29*, 425.

Hart, H. M. (1954). The relations between state and federal law. *Columbia Law Review*, *54*(4), 489–542.

Hasselmann, A. R. (2013). Successful strategies for recruitment of emergency medical volunteers. *Disaster Medicine and Public Health Preparedness*, *7*(3), 266–271.

Herman, M. L. (2021). Risk management. In K. Seel (Ed.), *Volunteer Administration: Professional Practice* (4th ed.). LexisNexis Canada.

Hidalgo, M. C., & Moreno, P. (2009). Organizational socialization of volunteers: The effect on their intention to remain. *Journal of Community Psychology*, *37*(5), 594–601.

Hirschfield, P. J., & Piquero, A. R. (2010). Normalization and legitimation: Modeling stigmatizing attitudes toward ex-offenders. *Criminology*, *48*(1), 27–55.

Hobson, C. J. (2007). The importance of initial assignment quality and staff treatment of new volunteers: A field test of the Hobson-Heler model of nonprofit agency "volunteer-friendliness." *International Journal of Volunteer Administration*, *14*(6), 47–56.

Hobson, C. J., Rominger, A., Malec, K., Hobson, C. L., & Evans, K. (1997). Volunteer-friendliness of nonprofit agencies: Definition, conceptual model, and applications. *Journal of Nonprofit & Public Sector Marketing*, *4*(4), 27–41.

Home Office. (1970). *Non-custodial and Semi-custodial Penalties: Report of the Advisory Council on the Penal System.* HMSO

Huebner, B. M., & Shannon, S. K. S. (2022). Private probation costs, compliance, and the proportionality of punishment: Evidence from Georgia and Missouri. *RSF: The Russell Sage Foundation Journal of the Social Sciences, 8*(1), 179–199. https://doi.org/10.7758/RSF.2022.8.1.08.

Huynh, J.-Y., Metzer, J. C., & Winefield, A. H. (2012). Engaged or connected? A perspective of the motivational pathway of the job demands-resources model in volunteers working for nonprofit organizations. *Voluntas: International Journal of Voluntary and Nonprofit Organizations, 23*, 870–898.

Illinois Criminal Justice Information Authority. (2011). *Examining Illinois Probationer Characteristics and Outcomes.* Illinois Criminal Justice Information Authority. www.jrsa.org/awards/winners/11_Illinois_Probationer_Characteristics.pdf.

Jackson, R., Locke, M., Hogg, E., & Lynch, R. (2019). *The Complete Volunteer Management Handbook* (4th ed.). Directory of Social Change.

Jamison, I. B. (2003). Turnover and retention among volunteers in human service agencies. *Review of Public Personnel Administration, 23*(2), 114–132.

Kaeble, D. (2018). *Probation and Parole in the United States, 2016* (NCJ 251148). Bureau of Justice Statistics, U.S. Department of Justice. www.bjs.gov/index.cfm?ty=pbdetail&iid=6188.

Killias, M., Aebi, M., & Ribeaud, D. (2000). Does community service rehabilitate better than short-term imprisonment?: Results of a controlled experiment. *The Howard Journal of Criminal Justice, 39*(1), 40–57.

Killias, M., Gilliéron, G., Kissling, I., & Villettaz, P. (2010). Community service versus electronic monitoring – What works better?: Results of a randomized trial. *The British Journal of Criminology, 50*(6), 1155–1170.

Killias, M., Gilliéron, G., Villard, F., & Poglia, C. (2010). How damaging is imprisonment in the long-term? A controlled experiment comparing long-term effects of community service and short custodial sentences on re-offending and social integration. *Journal of Experimental Criminology, 6*(2), 115–130.

Kim, M., Chelladurai, P., & Trail, G. T. (2007). A model of volunteer retention in youth sport. *Journal of Sport Management, 21*(2), 151–171. https://doi.org/10.1123/jsm.21.2.151.

Klein, A. (1982). The theater connection. *Training Manual for a Court Employment and Training Program, Governors Youth Grant.* Quincey District Court.

Klingele, C. (2013). Rethinking the use of community supervision. *Journal of Criminal Law and Criminology, 103*, 1015.

Knapp, M., Robertson, E., & McIvor, G. (1992). The comparative costs of community service and custody in Scotland. *The Howard Journal of Criminal Justice, 31*(1), 8–30.

Kolnick, L., & Mulder, J. (2007). Strategies to improve recruitment of male volunteers in nonprofit agencies. *American Journal of Hospice & Palliative Medicine, 24*(2), 98–104.

Kulik, L. (2006). Burnout among volunteers in the social services: The impact of gender and employment status. *Journal of Community Psychology, 34*(5), 541–561.

Kyrwood, D. L., & Meneghetti, M. M. (2010). Volunteer staffing and development. In K. Seel (Ed.), *Volunteer Administration: Professional Practice* (pp. 143–209). LexisNexis Canada.

Lloyd, C., Mair, G., & Hough, J. M. (1994). *Explaining Reconviction Rates: A Critical Analysis*. HM Stationery Office.

MacDuff, N. (2012). Volunteer and staff relations. In T. D. Connors (Ed.), *The Volunteer Management Handbook: Leadership Strategies for Success* (2nd ed., pp. 206–221). John Wiley & Sons.

Machin, J., & Paine, A. E. (2008). *Management Matters: A National Survey of Volunteer Management Capacity*. Institute for Volunteering Research.

Mair, G., & Canton, R. (2007). Sentencing, community penalties and the role of the Probation Service. In L. Gelsthorpe, R. Morgan (Eds.), *Handbook of Probation* (248–291). Willan.

May, C. (1999). *Explaining Reconviction Following a Community Sentence: The Role of Social Factors*. Home Office London.

Mayr, M. L. (2017). Transformational leadership and volunteer firefighter engagement. *Nonprofit Management and Leadership, 28*(2), 259–270. https://doi.org/10.1002/nml.21279.

McDonald, D. (1986). *Punishment without Walls: Community Service Sentences in New York City*. Rutgers University Press.

McDonald, D. (1988). *Restitution and Community Service*. US Department of Justice, National Institute of Justice.

McIvor, G. (1992). *Sentenced to Serve: The Operation and Impact of Community Service by Offenders*. Avebury.

McIvor, G. (1993a). Community service by offenders: Agency experiences and attitudes. *Research on Social Work Practice, 3*(1), 66–82. https://doi.org/10.1177/104973159300300104.

McIvor, G. (1993b). Community service by offenders: How much does the community benefit? *Research on Social Work Practice, 3*(4), 385–403. https://doi.org/10.1177/104973159300300402.

McIvor, G. (2016). What is the impact of community service? In F. MacNeill, I. Durnescu, & R. Butter (Eds.), *Probation: 12 Essential Questions* (pp. 107–128). Palgrave Macmillan.

McIvor, G., Beyens, K., Blay, E., & Boone, M. (2010). Community service in Belgium, the Netherlands, Scotland and Spain: A comparative perspective. *European Journal of Probation, 2*(1), 82–98.

Meijs, L., & Brudney, J. L. (2007). Winning volunteer scenarios: The soul of a new machine. *International Journal of Volunteer Administration, 24*(6), 68–79.

Miles, M. B., Huberman, A. M., & Saldaña, J. (2020). *Qualitative Data Analysis: A Methods Sourcebook* (Griffin Georgia Experiment Station H62 .M437 2020; 4th ed.). SAGE.

Mitchell, S.-L., & Clark, M. (2020). Volunteer choice of nonprofit organisation: An integrated framework. *European Journal of Marketing, 55*(1), 63–94. https://doi.org/10.1108/EJM-05-2019-0427.

Muiluvuori, M.-L. (2001). Recidivism among people sentenced to community service in Finland. *Journal of Scandinavian Studies in Criminology & Crime Prevention, 2*(1), 72–82. https://doi.org/10.1080/140438501317205556.

Nesbit, R. (2024). Leading and managing volunteers. In D. O. Renz, W. A. Brown, & F. Andersson (Eds.), *The Jossey-Bass Handbook of Nonprofit Leadership and Management* (5th ed., pp. 679–716). Jossey-Bass.

Office of Justice Research and Performance. (2016). *Executive Law Article 13-A Classification/Alternatives to Incarceration Program 2015 Annual Report* (Legislative Report Series). Division of Criminal Justice Services. www.crim inaljustice.ny.gov/crimnet/ojsa/Annual-13A-Legislative-Report-2015.pdf.

Pearce, J. L. (1993). *Volunteers: The Organizational Behavior of Unpaid Workers*.

Pease, K. (1985). Community service orders. *Crime and Justice, 6*, 51–94.

Phelps, M. S. (2013). The Paradox of probation: Community supervision in the age of mass incarceration: The paradox of probation. *Law & Policy, 35*(1–2), 51–80. https://doi.org/10.1111/lapo.12002.

Phelps, M. S. (2020). Mass probation from micro to macro: Tracing the expansion and consequences of community supervision. *Annual Review of Criminology, 3*(1), 261–279. https://doi.org/10.1146/annurev-criminol-011419-041352.

Prince, W., & Piatak, J. (2022). By the volunteer, for the volunteer: Volunteer perspectives of management across levels of satisfaction. *Nonprofit and Voluntary Sector Quarterly, 52*(5), 1191–1209. https://doi.org/10.1177/08997640221127974.

Rehnborg, S. J., Bailey, W. L., Moore, M., & Sinatra, C. (2009). Strategic volunteer engagement: A guide for nonprofit and public sector leaders. *RGK Center for Philanthropy & Community Service*. https://www.volunteer alive.org/docs/Strategic%20Volunteer%20Engagement.pdf.

Rex, S., & Gelsthorpe, L. (2002). The role of community service in reducing offending: Evaluating Pathfinder projects in the UK. *The Howard Journal of Criminal Justice, 41*(4), 311–325.

Rimes, H., Nesbit, R., Christensen, R. K., & Brudney, J. L. (2017). Exploring the dynamics of volunteer and staff interactions. *Nonprofit Management and Leadership, 28*(2), 195–213. https://doi.org/10.1002/nml.21277.

Rogelberg, S. G., Allen, J. A., Conway, J. M., et al. (2010). Employee experiences with volunteers. *Nonprofit Management and Leadership, 20*(4), 423–444. https://doi.org/10.1002/nml.20003.

Rubin, A. T. (2015). A neo-institutional account of prison diffusion. *Law & Society Review, 49*(2), 365–400. https://doi.org/10.1111/lasr.12136.

Saldaña, J. (2016). *The Coding Manual for Qualitative Researchers* (Griffin Georgia Experiment Station H62 .S343 2016; 3E.). SAGE.

Schiff, M. (2003). Models, promises and the promise of restorative justice strategies. In A. Von Hirsch, J. Roberts, A. E. Bottoms, K. Roach, & M. Schiff (Eds.), *Restorative Justice and Criminal Justice: Competing or Reconcilable Paradigms* (pp. 315–338). Hart.

Schneider, S. K., & George, W. M. (2011). Servant leadership versus transformational leadership in voluntary service organizations. *Leadership & Organization Development Journal, 32*(1), 60–77. https://doi.org/10.1108/01437731111099283.

Schreiner, E., Trent, S. B., Prange, K. A., & Allen, J. A. (2018). Leading volunteers: Investigating volunteers' perceptions of leaders' behavior and gender. *Nonprofit Management and Leadership, 29*(2), 241–260. https://doi.org/10.1002/nml.21331.

Shichor, D. (2000). Penal policies at the threshold of the twenty-first century. *Criminal Justice Review, 25*(1), 1–30. https://doi.org/10.1177/073401680002500103.

Spaans, E. C. (1998). Community service in the Netherlands: Its effects on recidivism and net-widening. *International Criminal Justice Review, 8*(1), 1–14. https://doi.org/10.1177/105756779800800101.

Studer, S. (2016). Volunteer management: Responding to the uniqueness of volunteers. *Nonprofit and Voluntary Sector Quarterly, 45*(4), 688–714.

Stukas, A. A., Worth, K. A., Clary, E. G., & Snyder, M. (2009). The matching of motivations to affordances in the volunteer environment: An index for assessing the impact of multiple matches on volunteer outcomes. *Nonprofit and Voluntary Sector Quarterly, 38*(1), 5–28. https://doi.org/10.1177/0899764008314810.

Teegardin, C. (2015, November 19). Georgia leads nation in probation. *The Atlanta Journal-Constitution.* www.ajc.com/news/crime–law/georgia-leads-nation-probation/4DgAXu3UHx5716BmSfYLVP/.

Tonry, M. (1999). Community penalties in the United States. *European Journal on Criminal Policy and Research*, 7(1), 5–22. https://doi.org/10.1023/A:1008755227099.

Tonry, M., & Lynch, M. (1996). Intermediate sanctions. *Crime and Justice: A Review of Research*, 20, 99.

Uggen, C., Manza, J., & Behrens, A. (2004). Less than the average citizen: Stigma, role transition and the civic reintegration of convicted felons. In S. Maruna & R. Immarigeon (Eds.), *After Crime and Punishment: Pathways to Offender Reintegration* (pp. 261–293). Willan. https://doi.org/10.4324/9781843924203.

Uggen, C., Vuolo, M., Lageson, S., Ruhland, E., & Whitham, H. K. (2014). The edge of stigma: An experimental audit of the effects of low-level criminal records on employment. *Criminology*, 52(4), 627–654.

United States Sentencing Commisison. (2023). *Guidelines Manual §3E1.1*. https://www.ussc.gov/sites/default/files/pdf/guidelines-manual/2023/GLMFull.pdf.

UPS Foundation. (2002). *A Guide to Investing in Volunteer Resources Management: Improve Your Philanthropic Portfolio*. Points of Light Foundation and Volunteer Center National Network. www.ellisarchive.org/sites/default/files/2019-08/Document_20190806_0003_2.pdf.

Van Schie, S., Güntert, S. T., Oostlander, J., & Wehner, T. (2015). How the organizational context impacts volunteers: A differentiated perspective on self-determined motivation. *Voluntas: International Journal of Voluntary and Nonprofit Organizations*, 26, 1570–1590.

Wandersman, A., & Alderman, J. (1993). Incentives, costs, and barriers for volunteers: A staff perspective on volunteers in one state. *Review of Public Personnel Administration*, 13(1), 67–76. https://doi.org/10.1177/0734371X9301300106.

Wermink, H., Blokland, A., Nieuwbeerta, P., Nagin, D., & Tollenaar, N. (2010). Comparing the effects of community service and short-term imprisonment on recidivism: A matched samples approach. *Journal of Experimental Criminology*, 6(3), 325–349.

Wisner, P. S., Stringfellow, A., Youngdahl, W. E., & Parker, L. (2005). The service volunteer – loyalty chain: An exploratory study of charitable not-for-profit service organizations. *Journal of Operations Management*, 23(2), 143–161. https://doi.org/10.1016/j.jom.2004.07.003.

Wood, W. R. (2012). Correcting community service: From work crews to community work in a juvenile court. *Justice Quarterly*, 29(5), 684–711. https://doi.org/10.1080/07418825.2011.576688.

Cambridge Elements ☰

Public and Nonprofit Administration

Andrew Whitford

University of Georgia

Andrew Whitford is Alexander M. Crenshaw Professor of Public Policy in the School
of Public and International Affairs at the University of Georgia. His research centers on
strategy and innovation in public policy and organization studies.

Robert Christensen

Brigham Young University

Robert Christensen is professor and George Romney Research Fellow in the Marriott
School at Brigham Young University. His research focuses on prosocial and antisocial
behaviors and attitudes in public and nonprofit organizations.

About the Series

The foundation of this series are cutting-edge contributions on emerging topics
and definitive reviews of keystone topics in public and nonprofit administration,
especially those that lack longer treatment in textbook or other formats.
Among keystone topics of interest for scholars and practitioners of public and
nonprofit administration, it covers public management, public budgeting and finance,
nonprofit studies, and the interstitial space between the public and nonprofit
sectors, along with theoretical and methodological contributions, including
quantitative, qualitative and mixed-methods pieces.

The Public Management Research Association

The Public Management Research Association improves public governance by advancing
research on public organizations, strengthening links among interdisciplinary scholars, and
furthering professional and academic opportunities in public management.

Cambridge Elements ≡

Public and Nonprofit Administration

Elements in the Series

A full series listing is available at: www.cambridge.org/EPNP

Printed in the United States
by Baker & Taylor Publisher Services